MW01127212

WHY THE UNITED STATES IS A MORALLY GOOD COUNTRY

A View from the Center

WHY THE UNITED STATES IS A MORALLY GOOD COUNTRY
A View from the Center

PHIL KERSHNER

dragon tree books

Published by

1620 SW 5th Avenue
Pompano Beach, Florida 33060
(954)788-4775
editors@editingforauthors.com
dragontreebooks.com

*To Sandee, Ashlyn, and Lauren, without whom
life would not seem good in any country.*

*And to my beloved professor, Peggy Way, who
always urged me to follow the yellow brick road of evidence,
wherever it led.*

If there's a book you want to read, but it hasn't been written yet, then you must write it.

—*Toni Morrison*

Contents

Introduction

What makes for a good country? I am thinking of moral good—winning gold medals at the Olympics or having the best pizza is not what I have in mind. I suspect if you asked one hundred people what they think makes for a good country, no two lists would be identical, but there would be a great deal of overlap.

I don't claim to have some kind of definitive list, but I will in these chapters explore various qualities and achievements of this nation that I believe most people would agree are morally good ("morally good" being generally understood here as affirming and contributing toward human betterment). I am happy to say that I believe there are many good countries in the world (as well as some that are not good and some that are in that grey area). Of course, no country fully embodies every aspect of the good. So how does one answer the question posed at the beginning of this introduction? Perhaps the same way one would make the same decision about an individual: one looks for enough evidence of the good to tip the balance in a positive direction.

I believe the United States is in that group of good countries. If, as you think about this country, you are drawn toward its negatives (and they certainly exist), I hope to provide you with enough evidence of moral goodness to tip the balance positively. Perhaps for many of you, the idea that the U.S. is a good country is quite obvious. Sadly, I have seen enough from those who think otherwise to lead me to think that the idea that the U.S. is a good country needs to be defended. The inspiration for this book was a July 4, 2016 statement from my religious denomination, the United Church of Christ, in which Traci Blackmon (one of the denomination's national leaders) suggested that the crack in the Liberty Bell—and the subsequent silence of the bell—is a fitting metaphor for a country in which, she said, "Freedom cannot ring." She added, "The Liberty Bell, its inscription and its breach, serve to remind us that freedom is often proclaimed yet seldom advanced..."[1]

Bashing the U.S. is practically a cottage industry among many in the UCC's national leadership. But the suggestion that there is nothing for which to ring the bell (or that freedom is seldom advanced in this country) demanded a response. A year and a half after that statement came out, I started to write this book to demonstrate the lack of moral imagination exhibited by Blackmon and those who think like her. There is, indeed, a great deal that is good about the United States, a truth that we shall see rings loudly for many around the world.

Politically, I consider myself something of a centrist with some libertarian leanings. I have often told people that two of the great issues we dealt with in the twentieth century were Soviet totalitarianism and the civil rights movement of the mid-twentieth century. I believe the left was wrong about the former and correct about the latter. I believe the right was correct about the former and wrong about the latter. The same could be said about other issues. I believe the left was correct about gay rights. I believe the right was correct about what the welfare state would do to families (although, interestingly, that case may have been best made by the liberal New York Senator, Daniel Patrick Moynihan). That this should be so makes perfect intuitive sense. What is the probability that one side could be right *all the time*?

I am not an "American exceptionalist." It is not my position that the U.S. is the greatest country in the history of the world, or even the greatest country at the present moment. I am happy to say that most of my fellow citizens in the U.S. are not American exceptionalists either. A 2014 Pew Research Poll found that only 28 percent of Americans believe that the U.S. is the greatest country in the world (down sharply from 38 percent in 2011), while 58 percent believe it is one of the great countries of the world (a reasonable belief that this book will defend). Furthermore, any remaining belief in American exceptionalism is becoming less common. The age group most inclined to believe that the U.S. is the greatest country was those sixty-five years of age and older (40 percent), while only 15 percent of those under thirty held that belief.[2]

There are many good countries in this world (I prefer to use the word "good" rather than "great," but I don't draw a line in the sand over the issue). I believe the U.S. is among them, but I find it a foolish endeavor to try to take the position that any of them is the greatest. How would you even go about establishing such a thesis? What are the criteria? I believe the chapters in this book are so far-ranging and varied in scope that they would defeat any attempt to select certain criteria as the "key" ones. And even if you could, how do you compare a country of 323 million racially diverse people (the U.S.) with a country like Denmark, with a population of just under six million racially homogeneous people?

I believe that racial diversity is a good thing. But let's not kid ourselves. Humans have evolved to be wary of "otherness," and differences of race or color or ethnicity are among those that have plagued us the most in recent centuries. This is the elephant in the room. We have to talk about it, even though it is not an issue in many of the chapters of this book. The U.S. is 61.3 percent white. The western European nations, plus Canada and Australia, to which we are most often compared, are generally 80–95 percent white (with most of them well above 80 percent). To suggest this makes no difference is to bury one's head in the sand. There are racial problems in Canada and Britain and France and Germany and most of these largely white nations, but they don't get the attention that racial problems receive in the U.S. because these other countries have far fewer people of color (in raw numbers and, more importantly, as a percentage of their populations).

Let me give two examples. It is well known that in the U.S., blacks are in prison in numbers disproportionate to the percentage of the population they make up. Blacks make up 13.3 percent of the U.S. population, but 37.8 percent of its federal prison population and 38 percent of its state prison population (a ratio slightly less than three-to-one).[3] That's a real problem. But look who has a bigger problem. The ratio in Canada is slightly *more* than three-to-one.[4] And in the UK, the ratio is four-to-one.[5] This gets far less attention. I couldn't find figures for Germany, but I did find this, written by the legal journalist Andrew Hammel:

> If you define an ethnic minority in Germany the way most legal systems do—someone whose external appearance is different from the native population and who has been the victim of discrimination by the majority native population—then the number of ethnic minorities in German prisons, I am sure, would be at least 50 percent. There are no reliable statistics I have yet seen to prove this, *because Germany doesn't keep them* (see no evil, hear no evil, speak no evil). But I've visited many German criminal courts,

talked to cops, prosecutors, and defense lawyers, and been to German prisons. Everybody recognizes the vast over-representation of ethnic minorities in German prisons as an everyday fact of life that only the most reality-resistant Green Party ideologue would ever contest. I am happy to be corrected on this, but nobody has so far succeeded.[6]

This is in a country in which only 9.5 percent of the population are ethnic minorities[7]—without the qualifier of having been a victim of discrimination.

Hammel's difficulty in finding information about issues of race in Germany is not unusual for Europe. European nations, for the most part, do not share (or even collect) such information. The U.S. is perhaps the most transparent nation when it comes to airing our dirty laundry (I suppose that could have been on my list of things to celebrate about the U.S.). Yet journalists like Hammel have often been able to get past the government censorship of race and ethnicity data to see what is really going on in the rest of the developed world.

A second example: in 2015, the black and minority (BME) unemployment rate in Britain was 9.9 percent.[8] In the U.S., it was significantly less. U.S. figures are given by individual groups rather than as a whole. But the *highest* rate of any group in the U.S. in 2015 was 9.9 percent (i.e., equal to the overall rate for the British). That was the unemployment rate for Native Americans. For blacks, the rate was 9.6 percent, for Hispanics it was 6.6 percent, and for Asian Americans it was 3.8 percent.[9] Clearly, the overall rate for the U.S. was significantly below that of Britain.

Please understand, this is not about being black or white or any other color. This is about diversity. It is not that being white makes for lesser problems. It is homogeneity that is the issue, not color (see my comments on Botswana in Chapter 8). Take, for example, the issue of homicide rates. There are countries in Asia, Africa, and South America with homicide rates lower than the U.S. and comparable to many European countries. These countries are clearly not white, but they are largely homogeneous. They do not have the racial diversity that the U.S. has. Let us not pretend that, for all its beauty, diversity does not present difficulties. I will usually use the term "racial diversity" in this book, but please understand that I am including within that framework "ethnic diversity." I see no need here to parse them out. What I am doing is no different than what people are doing when they speak of "people of color" (a term I also use). When they speak of people of color, they are including, among others, a race, namely the black race, and an ethnic group, Hispanics.

The psychologist Jonathan Haidt, in his book *The Righteous Mind: Why Good People are Divided by Politics and Religion*, examines the difficulties brought about by diversity. Haidt (named by *Foreign Policy* magazine as one of the "top global thinkers") has himself moved from somewhere pretty far to the left to somewhere pretty close to the center:

> John Lennon captured a common liberal theme in his haunting song "Imagine." Imagine if there were no countries, and no religions too. If we could just erase the borders and boundaries that divide us, then the world would "be as one." It's a vision of heaven for liberals, but conservatives believe it would quickly descend into hell. I think conservatives are on to something.
>
> Throughout this book I've argued that large-scale human societies are nearly miraculous achievements. I've tried to show how our complicated moral psychology coevolved with our religion and our other cultural inventions (such

as tribes and agriculture) to get us to where we are today. I have argued that we are the products of multilevel selection, including group selection, and that our 'parochial altruism' is part of what makes us such great team players. We need groups, we love groups, and we develop our virtues in groups, even though these groups necessarily exclude non-members. If you destroy all groups and dissolve all internal structure, you destroy your moral capital.

...In a previous chapter I told you about his [Robert Putnam's] finding that religions make Americans into "better neighbors and better citizens.". ...Anything that binds people into dense networks of trust make people less selfish.

In an earlier study, Putnam found that ethnic diversity had the opposite effect. In a paper revealingly titled "E Pluribus Unum," Putnam examined the level of social capital in hundreds of American communities and discovered that high levels of immigration and ethnic diversity seem to cause a reduction in social capital. That may not surprise you; people are racist, you might think, and so they don't trust people who don't look like themselves. But that's not quite right. Putnam's survey was able to distinguish between two different kinds of social capital: *bridging capital* refers to trust between groups, between people who have different values and identities, while *bonding capital* refers to trust within groups. Putnam found that diversity reduced *both* kinds of social capital. Here's his conclusion: 'Diversity seems to trigger not in-group/out-group division, but anomie or social isolation. In colloquial language, people living in ethnically diverse settings appear to 'hunker down'—that is, to pull in like a turtle.' [My note: notice how Putnam himself moves seamlessly from talking about ethnicity to talking about race.]

Putnam uses Durkheim's ideas (such as anomie) to explain why diversity makes people turn inward and become more selfish, less interested in contributing to their communities...[10]

I believe we will someday find a way to overcome (or at least minimize) these problems, but in the meantime, I believe so strongly in the value of diversity that I am willing to put up with its drawbacks in order to enjoy its benefits. Why? As a white person who grew up in the Los Angeles area, I shamelessly admit to being the ultimate cliché. My best friend in grade school was a Hispanic boy who lived across the street. My best friend in the multi-ethnic, multi-racial high school I attended was Asian American. Having spent all my adult life living halfway across the country, I have not kept in close contact with any of my high school friends, but the ones with whom I have had the most contact (admittedly not much) are black. I now happen to live in a very white area in southern Illinois, but still treasure growing up in the diversity of Los Angeles and going to college in the diversity of Chicago.

The situation described above by Putnam is not irreversible. Several years ago a former U.S. president recognized both the challenge of diversity and the possibility of change.

After the August 2014 shooting of Michael Brown in Ferguson, Missouri, President Obama spoke of the need for the U.S. to continue to deal with the racial issues that challenge us. But he also said this: "We have made enormous progress in race relations over the course of the past several decades. I've witnessed that in my own life. And to deny that progress, I think, is to deny America's capacity for change." I believe he was right on both counts.

Furthermore, the racism that needs to be challenged is not only found among Hillary Clinton's "deplorables." The conservative economist Walter Williams writes about a type of racism that is largely found among our intellectual elites. In 2000, he wrote, "In fact, it's fairly safe to say that most of today's most flagrant human rights abuses occur in Africa. But unfortunately they get little attention—maybe it's because Africans instead of Europeans are the perpetrators; Europeans are held accountable to civilized standards of behavior while Africans aren't."[11] That which Williams describes may be the most insidious form of racism because it is more subtle than outright forms of racism. It devalues the dignity of the other. It presumes the other is not up to your standards of morality.

What I have tried to do in this book is find morally compelling reasons to support the thesis that the United States is a good country. I suspect many will be surprised by many of my reasons. They may be things you have never known or never given much thought to. Take a look at Chapter 1, for example. The data given there has surprised nearly everyone to whom I have shown it.

I am not an authority on the topics covered. In some cases, I was able to find the relevant information and draw conclusions largely on my own. But in several chapters I have relied on the expertise of others.

Could one write a book on morally compelling reasons to consider Canada or Denmark or Botswana or Chile or (name your country) a good country? Of course, but that will have to be someone else's project. Could one write a book on morally compelling problems that plague the U.S.? Of course, but that will also have to be someone else's project (although I certainly touch on some of those problems in this book; indeed, I already have). I do not believe the evils of our past prevent us from saying this is a good country. I would certainly say that Germany is a good country, even though less than seventy-five years ago the Germans were killing millions of Jews and others. I would certainly say that Sweden is a good country, even though they sat out World War II and made money selling iron ore to the Germans throughout the war. I would certainly say that Switzerland is a good country, even though they also sat out World War II while their famed banking business made money dealing with the Germans. I would certainly say that Britain is a good country despite their history of engaging in the slave trade and in colonization. Furthermore, I would say that all these countries, including the U.S., are good countries in spite of present-day evils.

The data I have used is the most recent I could find at the time I was writing (late 2017 into mid-2018). You may be able to find somewhat different data at the time of your reading, but I doubt it will substantially change much of the argument I am making.

1

Life Expectancy

One criteria often used to measure the well-being of a country is its life expectancy (note: as I will argue below, life expectancy is *not* a good measure of a country's health system, but that is not the issue here). Not long ago, I got to thinking about the life expectancy of various groups *within* this country. I discovered something about the U.S. that, to be honest, shocked me. If you asked one hundred people to guess whether white people or people of color in the U.S. have the longer life expectancy, I suspect ninety or more would guess white people. They would be wrong. As astonishing as this may sound, the life expectancy of people of color in the U.S. is greater than that of white people. I found the following figures for population and life expectancy for people of color in the United States: There are 4.2 million Native Americans[12] with a life expectancy of 75.1 years.[13] There are 18.4 million Asian Americans[14] with a life expectancy of 86.7 years.[15]

I

There are 43.0 million black Americans[16] with a life expectancy of 75.6 years.[17] And there are 57.5 million Hispanic Americans[18] with a life expectancy of 82.9 years.[19]

Of course, you can't find the average life expectancy for people of color by simply averaging the four life expectancy figures given above. You must do a weighted average. If you multiply the number of people in each of the four groups by the life expectancy for each group, then add those four products together and divide by the total population of people of color, you will get a life expectancy of 80.7 for people of color. The life expectancy for white Americans is 79.1.[20] Now, there are some who would say we shouldn't include Asian Americans. Why they would say that I don't understand, but even if you remove the Asian Americans from the above calculations and do the math again, the cherry-picked results will still end up with people of color on top: a life expectancy of 79.6, half a year longer than the life expectancy for white people. I would challenge anyone to find a white-majority developed country where the people of color are anywhere nearly as diversified as they are in the U.S., in which it is also true that people of color live longer than white people.

Two interesting footnotes to this data: The life expectancy for blacks in this country was seven years short of the life expectancy for whites as recently as 1999. By 2015, that differential had been cut in half.[21] The current differential between Native Americans and whites (four years) is a huge improvement over the twenty-four-year differential back in 1974.[22]

Is the fact that people of color have a longer life expectancy than white Americans a moral good? I believe it is. It is a sign of the tremendous progress that has been made toward overcoming a long history of ugly racism in this country. Those on the right who deny that racism still exists are wrong. But equally wrong are those on the left who suggest that people of color live under a systemic and oppressive system of racism foisted on them by white people. It strains credulity to believe that in such a systemic and oppressive system, the oppressed would outlive the oppressors.

Jews in Germany in the 1930s were victims of a systemic and oppressive system (and later, of course, of genocide). Blacks in South Africa under apartheid were victims of systemic and oppressive racism. Blacks in this country, living in the era of Jim Crow, were victims of systemic and oppressive racism. Racism is still real, but to call every expression of it systemic and oppressive is to make the term "racism" problematic. It also makes meaningless the words spoken by Obama (and quoted in the introduction) about the enormous progress made in this country with regard to race relations, and about America's capacity for change. And, finally, it makes it difficult to square with information we will see in later chapters. For example, in chapter 11 we will see that black Americans and white Americans have virtually the same sense of satisfaction with life, and black Americans are significantly more optimistic about the future than are white Americans. If some whites are less optimistic because they see newspaper articles indicating that within less than three decades the U.S. will no longer be a white-majority nation, the loss is theirs. Fifty years from now this country will be a better place than it is now. It's not too late to get on board.

CHAPTER 2

Voting with Their Hearts
and With Their Feet

In a poll taken between 2013 and 2016 covering 156 countries (representing 98 percent of the world's population), Gallup found that 14 percent of adults would move to another country if they had the opportunity. And given the choice, what would be the number one preferred country of destination for those wishing to emigrate? Beautiful and wealthy Switzerland? One of the very progressive and highly educated Scandinavian countries? Environmentally green and manufacturing powerhouse Germany? No, none of those. The number one choice of destination was the United States. And it wasn't even close. The U.S. was chosen by more than three times as many people as the number two country (Germany). In fact, the U.S. was picked by more people than the next four countries (Germany, Canada, the UK, and France) combined.[23]

I wouldn't call this "voting with their feet" since those polled haven't actually moved (yet). But I would call it "voting with their hearts." In a discussion with an Australian who feels great disdain for the U.S., my mention of this poll brought the retort that people around the world are attracted to the U.S. because they see our movies. Trying hard to subdue my inclination to break out laughing, I merely pointed out that movies have been around for about a century and if the picture they presented of the U.S. was that far out of touch with reality, I suspect word would have gotten back to the rest of the world by now.

Of course, there are some who have voted with their feet. In the following chapter we will see that the majority of those coming to the U.S. come from poor nations (which I think is to our credit). But we do get a fair number from developed countries. The *Chicago Tribune* published an article in January 2018 showing that the number of Americans going to Norway is greater than the number of Norwegians coming to the U.S. The *Tribune's* mathematical literacy leaves much to be desired. Here is the crucial data from the article titled, "More Americans migrated to Norway than the other way around in 2016": "In 2016, however, only 1,114 Norwegians moved to the U.S., while 1,603 Americans moved to Norway."[24] Yes, more Americans did indeed move to Norway than Norwegians moved to America. But 1,114 Norwegians represents 0.02 percent of their population, while 1,603 Americans represents .0005 percent of our population. That means that Norwegians are forty times more likely to come here than we are to go there. Did you get that impression from the headline or from the statement in the article?

Interestingly, a Canadian publication, using ten-year-old data (the most recent I could find), pegged the number of Americans living abroad at a mere 1.7 percent. They gave the number of Canadians living abroad at 8.8 percent (about one-third of them in the U.S.). Here were the figures they gave for some other developed countries: France, 3.3 percent; Australia, 4.3 percent; Britain, 9 percent; and New Zealand, 21.9 percent.[25] Elsewhere, I found that the number of Swedes living abroad is above 7 percent, and their favorite country of destination is the U.S.[26] I also found that 9.2 percent of Swiss citizens live abroad, with the U.S. trailing only France and Germany (both of which border Switzerland) as the favorite destination.[27] And, finally, I found that the U.S. is the second favorite destination of those Australians living abroad, only slightly trailing the UK. Moreover, the number of Americans living in Australia is 0.03 percent of the U.S. population. The percentage of Australians living in the U.S. is 0.39 percent of the Australian population. So Australians are thirteen times more likely to live here than we are to live there.[28]

The numbers in the above two paragraphs suggest an awful lot of "voting with their feet" is going on. And those feet are coming to the U.S. in much greater numbers than they are going the other way.

Does all this data indicate a moral good? I believe it does. Surely it is a moral good to have developed a country to which so many people around the world (both in the developed and undeveloped world) would want to immigrate if they had the opportunity, and to which so many do when they do have the opportunity.

Immigration: Who Is Doing the Most Good for the World?

In a piece lacking any kind of serious analysis, NPR reported in October 2014 that the U.S. was not a very generous country in terms of the number of immigrants living here.[29] The piece begins with the following bit of poor logic: "If you think the United States is every immigrant's dream, reconsider. Sure, in absolute numbers, the U.S. is home to the most foreign-born people—45.7 million in 2013.

> But *relatively*, it's upper-midpack as an immigrant nation. It ranks 65th worldwide in terms of percentage of population that is foreign-born, according to the U.N. report 'Trends in International Migrant Stock.'[30]

There is no logical connection between what an immigrant might dream of and where they end up, anymore than there is a logical connection between where high school graduates might dream of going to college and where they actually end up. The article is about the percentage of population that is foreign-born in various nations. That has nothing to do with "If you think the U.S. is every immigrant's dream, reconsider." The fact that 13.8 percent of the Spanish population is foreign-born tells us nothing about where those immigrants dreamed of going. And no sane person would think that the U.S. is *every* immigrant's dream, but as we saw in the previous chapter, more people would want to move to the U.S. than to any other country by a margin of more than three-to-one.

Before we go any further, we need to clarify some terminology. In a sense, of course, we are all immigrants. But when that term is used in this chapter, it means those who were born in one country and then moved to a different country. To emphasize this understanding I usually, though not always, will use the term "foreign-born." In both the second and third paragraphs of this chapter, NPR used both "immigrant" and "foreign-born" in the same paragraph. The terms are interchangeable both in the NPR piece and in this chapter.

The previously described logical fallacy aside, the more serious problem with the article is that it names a lot of countries which have a higher percentage of foreign-born people than does the U.S. without analyzing where those foreign-born people come from. Perhaps NPR was concerned that it would undercut their agenda. It is important to understand in what follows that when I talk about the source of a country's immigrants, I am not talking about where immigrants came from last year, or the year before, or even over the last ten years. I am talking about the country of origin for all of the foreign-born citizens (or permanent residents) in a given country.

The NPR article first looks at the percentage of foreign-born people making up the populations of Australia (27.7 percent), New Zealand (25.1 percent), and Canada (20.7 percent). All these, we are informed, exceed the 14.3 percent figure for the United States. But there are some inconvenient facts of which we are not informed by NPR (the importance of this information will become obvious when we look at the parallel information for the U.S.). The top two sources of foreign-born people in Australia (2015–16 data) have been the UK and New Zealand (Italy and Germany are also in the top ten).[31] That doesn't mean that in 2015–16 more people came to Australia from the UK than from anywhere else (in that time period, it's entirely possible that more came from China). It means, rather, that of all the foreign-born Australians in 2015–16, more had come from the UK than from anywhere else. The largest source of foreign-born people in New Zealand (2013 data) has been the UK (supplying more than 25 percent of New Zealand's foreign-born people) and the fourth largest source has been Australia.[32] The fourth, fifth, and sixth largest sources of foreign-born people in Canada (2016 data) have been the UK, the U.S., and Italy (narrowly missing the top ten were Poland, Germany, and Portugal in eleventh, twelfth, and thirteenth).[33] So where has the foreign-born population of the U.S. come from? According to the U.S. Census Bureau, here are the top ten feeder nations (2016 data): Mexico, India, China, the Philippines, El Salvador, Vietnam, Cuba, Dominican Republic, South Korea, and Guatemala. If you want to go deeper, the next five, in order, are Canada, Jamaica, Columbia, the UK, and Haiti.[34] With the exceptions of Canada in eleventh and the UK in fourteenth, they are all nations consisting almost entirely of people of color, and more than half are poor or near-poor (and the top ten has no exceptions to this rule). So who is doing more good for the world when it comes to being a home for foreign-born people: Australia, New Zealand, Canada, or the U.S.? I think the answer is quite clear. [Note: NPR will move on to Europe next and tout the foreign-born figures of several countries that exceed that of the U.S. As I have done for the countries above, I go through NPR's list and show, country by country, that immigration in Europe is largely a matter of shuffling around fellow Europeans. I invite you to look at the data, but if you are a bit weary of data at this point you may want to skip down to the paragraph beginning "Gulf states..."]

NPR next moves to Europe, where they tout the foreign-born numbers for Sweden and Ireland (both at 15.9 percent, a little higher than the U.S. figure). But among the top ten countries from which Sweden has received its foreign-born people (2016 data), we find Finland (#1), Poland (#4), the former Yugoslavia (#6), Bosnia and Herzegovina (#8), and Germany (#9).[35] As for Ireland, among the top ten countries from which they have received their foreign-born people, only one (Brazil) is not a European nation (from 2016 census).[36] NPR also touts the fact that Ireland has played host to a surge of Muslims, who now make up 1.1 percent of Ireland's population. That just happens to be about the same percentage that Muslims make up of the U.S. population.

Next we hear about Croatia and Estonia. NPR fails to tell us that 90.4 percent of Croatians are Croats.[37] The Croatian War for Independence (1991–1995) displaced many Croats, and much of the immigration heralded by NPR is the result of displaced people returning. As for Estonia (for which NPR gives us no numbers), the following comes from Statistics Estonia:

> The situation in Estonia is somewhat exceptional, because after the restoration of independence, the people who had initially changed their place of residence within the

territory of one and the same country found themselves in a new situation—they had become foreign-origin population. Thus, the foreign-origin population in Estonia can be considered untypical.[38]

Thus, NPR even mentioning them (with no numbers) has little meaning. One of the sneakiest moves made by NPR is to try to move from percentage of population that is foreign-born to "larger net migration inflows." This term simply reflects how many more people are moving in than are moving out. Of course, a country with a small percentage of foreign-born people could have a larger net migration inflow for a period of time than a country with a much higher percentage of foreign-born people. For example, one of the countries listed as having a larger net migration inflow than the U.S. is Italy. The percentage of Italy's population that is foreign-born is not small, but at 9.4 percent, it is significantly less than that of the U.S. (14.3 percent). If they maintain this larger net migration inflow for an extended period, they could reach our foreign-born percentage. But that's a big "if." And, in any event, they would still be getting a large portion of their foreign-born people from fellow European nations.

Our immigrant percentage is higher than that of the following western European nations: Norway (13.8 percent), Spain (13.8 percent), the UK (12.4 percent), Germany (11.9 percent), the Netherlands (11.7 percent), France (11.6 percent), Iceland (10.7 percent), Belgium (10.4 percent), Denmark (9.9 percent), Italy (9.4 percent), Greece (8.9 percent), and Finland (5.4 percent). We trail Australia, New Zealand, and Canada, as discussed above. We also trail Switzerland (28.9 percent), but here is what the Migration Policy Institute has to say about the presence of foreign-born people in Switzerland: "Foreigners' sizeable share of the population sets Switzerland apart from other European countries...

of those 1.6 million foreign residents, 62.6 percent were from EU/EFTA countries, mainly Italy and Germany."[39] More than half of the rest were also from European countries. That MPI report is from 2009, but according to the Federal Statistics Office of Switzerland, nothing had really changed as of 2016. The permanent foreign-born resident population came largely from Italy, Germany, and Portugal.[40]

A European nation with just a slightly larger percentage of foreign-born people than the U.S. is Austria (15.2 percent). Its largest feeder nation is Germany. Serbia, Romania, and Bosnia and Herzegovina are also in the top five.[41] Foreign-born people make up 43.3 percent of Luxembourg's permanent residents, with the top five feeder nations being Portugal, France, Italy, Belgium, and Germany.[42] Foreign-born people make up 33.1 percent of Liechtenstein's permanent residents, with the top five feeder nations being Germany, Austria, Switzerland, Italy, and Turkey.[43]

The picture one gets of Europe is that the largest part of foreign-born population there is the shuffling around of fellow Europeans. NPR seems to have glossed over this fact.

Next we hear from NPR about Monaco at 64.2 percent. The top five feeder nations for Monaco are France, Italy, Great Britain, Belgium, and Switzerland.[44] Then we learn that Andorra comes in at 56.9 percent. What we aren't told is that Andorra is a playground for the super wealthy. If you wish to reside there and are a professional with an international business or have scientific, cultural, or sports reasons to be there, it will only cost you fifty thousand Euros. If you don't meet any of those criteria, it will cost you four hundred thousand Euros.[45] If you're looking for a country in which to vacation where you can rub shoulders with people from all walks of life, scratch Andorra off your list.

Gulf states like the United Arab Emirates, Qatar, Kuwait, and Bahrain have foreign-born populations of up to 83.7 percent. With the exception of Kuwait, they also all have terrible records when it comes to respecting human rights. Taking one last cheap shot at the United States, NPR shamelessly writes, "Resource-rich, these business-driven nations are hungry for migrant workers who, in the case of Qatar, are greeted by 'modern day slavery' working conditions. Though in some cases, advocates say, it's not so different in the United States." It would be hard to be more wrong. The following comes from the Global Slavery Index:

> The countries with the highest estimated prevalence of modern slavery by the proportion of their population are North Korea, Uzbekistan, Cambodia, India, and Qatar. In North Korea, there is pervasive evidence that government-sanctioned forced labour occurs in an extensive system of prison labour camps while North Korean women are subjected to forced marriage and commercial sexual exploitation in China and other neighbouring states. In Uzbekistan, the government continues to subject its citizens to forced labour in the annual cotton harvest...

> The countries with the lowest estimated prevalence of modern slavery by the proportion of their population are Luxembourg, Ireland, Norway, Denmark, Switzerland, Austria, Sweden, Belgium, the United States, Canada, Australia, and New Zealand. These countries generally have more economic wealth, score higher on government response, have low levels of conflict, and are politically stable with a willingness to combat modern slavery."[46]

That NPR could write (quoting unnamed "advocates"), compared to Qatar, "it's not so different in the United States" is obscene. Qatar is listed with four other countries for the highest estimated prevalence of modern slavery in the world today, while the United States is listed among the lowest.

I guess NPR didn't trouble themselves to see how bad the problem is in Europe (or maybe in their mindset, they couldn't imagine Europe having such a problem). In any event, they missed a telling article in the *Guardian*. There we learn that:

> Governments across Europe are in a state of confusion and denial over the extent of forced labour within their own borders, contributing to hundreds of thousands of people remaining trapped in exploited, unpaid and dangerous working conditions, according to a new report.
>
> In a study of the presence and extent of forced labour in nine European countries, the Joseph Rowntree Foundation (JRF) concludes that the continued failure to recognize and address deficiencies in the regulation of the labour market is leading to the entrapment of up to 880,000 people in the worst forms of exploitation.
>
> The foundation carried out extensive investigations into forced labour conditions in France, Germany, Italy, Ireland, Latvia, the Netherlands, Poland, Spain and Sweden.
>
> 'What surprised us all was how easily we found examples of forced labour in all the nine countries we chose to focus on,' says Nick Clark, senior research fellow at London Metropolitan University and the lead author of the JRF report, 'Detecting and Tackling Forced Labour in Europe.'

The cases uncovered in the JRF report included trafficking and forced labour in German strawberry fields, the exploitation of Moroccan and Tunisian seasonal workers in French agriculture, domestic servitude in Ireland, and Chinese migrants trapped in bonded labour in textile factories in Spain.

A further case, in Sweden, concerned Thai workers forced to pay off large debts to their traffickers by picking berries used in the global pharmaceutical and health-food industries.[47]

The mention of Sweden is perplexing, as they ranked among the least problematic countries in the world according to the Global Slavery Index. I don't have an answer to this dilemma except to suggest that this report was only looking at western European nations, and even the worst of their numbers may look quite small compared to the countries of the world looked at in the JRF report.

If you are thinking that the recent refugee tragedy changes the foreign-born numbers very much, it doesn't. Take Germany as an example. Unfortunately, the refugee numbers are all over the map and no one can keep track of how many are leaving. A high refugee estimate for Germany seems to be one million. Give them credit for their remarkable generosity (in fact, if I were writing this book about Germany, that is one of the things I would highlight). We'll just assume all will become citizens or permanent residents, which, of course, isn't the case. Their foreign-born percentage given the above is 11.9 percent. In a country of 82.7 million people, that gives you 9.8 million foreign-born people. Add one million to that number and to the total population and your foreign-born percentage rises from 11.9 percent to 12.9 percent (still less than that of the U.S.).

Take Sweden as another example. They have been recognized for taking in the most refugees per capita of any European country (and, indeed, they have been very generous; take a bow, Sweden). As with Germany, it is very difficult to get any kind of handle on the number of refugees taken in. The numbers are all over the map. But I took the highest estimate I could find for Sweden (190,000 in 2015). Estimates for 2016 were even harder to find, but it is clear that the number was down. The following, from a September 2016 article, is very suggestive:

> Sweden's deputy prime minister, Åsa Romson, was reduced to tears last year [i.e. already in 2015] when announcing stricter rules designed to deter refugees from coming to Sweden. 'It pains me that Sweden is no longer capable of receiving asylum seekers at the high level we do today,' Sweden's prime minister, Stefan Löfven, said at another press conference last year. 'We simply cannot do any more.'
>
> Last year, a group of asylum seekers was left to sleep outside in the cold as the Swedish Migration Agency struggled to find them suitable accommodation, unusual for a country with such a long history of hosting refugees. Refugees in Sweden now only receive temporary residence permits, while the right to family reunification is restricted. The country also stepped up border controls, doubling the number of officers patrolling the southern coast, where most refugees arrive.[48]

Just for the sake of argument, let us assume a number of 100,000 for 2016, which is probably a gross overestimate. I'm not including 2017 because the pipeline had dwindled dramatically by then. The population of Sweden is 9.9 million, and 15.9 percent are foreign-born. That's a total of approximately 1.6 million foreign-born people. Add 290,000 to the number of foreign-born people and to the population, and Sweden's foreign-born percentage rises from 15.9 percent to 18.5 percent. That assumes, of course, that all 290,000 become citizens. Many who want to won't, and many, in fact, have already left. And, in any event, neither for Germany nor for Sweden will it change the fact that most of their foreign-born population is still the shuffling around of fellow Europeans.

All in all, the U.S. record on receiving foreign-born people, taking into account where the foreign-born people are coming from, leaves one thinking that the answer to the question raised in the title of this chapter ("Immigration: Who Is Doing the Most Good for the World?") might well be the U.S. Is this a moral good? I believe it is.

Looking for Happiness?

The United Nations has surveyed the nations of the world to produce a happiness report periodically since 2012. The UN is not so naïve as to think they can simply call people and ask them, "Are you happy?" Their survey looks at six factors: income, healthy life expectancy, having someone to count on in times of trouble, generosity, freedom, and trust, with the latter measured by the absence of corruption in business and government.

The most recent report covered the years 2015–2017. Despite those being rather tumultuous years in the United States, this country ranked eighteenth of the 156 countries included in the rankings.[49] That was a drop of four places from the previous report. For a country as large and diverse as the U.S., I think that's a very good showing. Interestingly, the combined population of the seventeen countries ahead of us is 238.5 million. That is 74 percent of the U.S. population of 323 million. So I might again ask that same question, who is doing more good for the world? Such a high ranking for the U.S. would be mathematically highly unlikely in a nation in which 39 percent of the population are people of color (not to mention the percentage of the white population that is LGTBQ and/or poor) if said people were largely unhappy.

While I suspect few in the modern world would want to return to the days of hunter-gatherers, such societies did have certain advantages in being small. Smallness, of course, is not always an advantage, but it does make some human desires easier to achieve. In a group of 150, you are able to know everyone and feel more connected to your leaders. Obviously, no modern nation comes remotely close to such small size, but it is interesting to note that if you look at the ratio of citizens to the number of members in a country's national legislative body, the highest ratio of any country ahead of us in the happiness report is Australia's ratio of 160,000 citizens per member of the national legislative body. By contrast, in the U.S. there are 603,000 citizens per member of our national legislative body. Only three other countries of the seventeen ahead of us have a ratio greater than 100,000-to-one (the Netherlands, Germany, and Canada). Most of the rest are grouped between 25,000-to-one and 50,000-to-one. The four "happiest" nations (Finland, Norway, Denmark, and Iceland) have four of the seven lowest ratios. Of course, a small ratio doesn't guarantee happiness. There are many nations that rank very low in happiness which also have low ratios. Sadly, their governments are rife with corruption, and these countries suffer a great deal of civil strife and other problems. But while a low ratio can certainly not guarantee happiness, I suspect it may contribute to it if the other needed parameters are in place. When you feel more connection to those who lead your country, there is a stronger likelihood of the kind of trust developing that is one of the UN's six criteria.

While these numbers are interesting, I suspect a small population has even more to do with happiness than having a relatively small ratio of citizens to national legislators. It is interesting to scan through the list of the top forty countries (which is roughly the top 25 percent of the list) and notice that only one, Brazil, has even half our population. But even a small population is no guarantee of happiness. There are many small countries near the bottom of the list. Sadly, these countries have few of the institutions and traditions in place that make for happiness.

I have emphasized that neither a small ratio of citizens to national legislators nor a small population can guarantee happiness. The situation is a bit analogous to that of natural resources. An abundance of such resources can certainly help a country to achieve greater happiness (not because wealth brings happiness, but because most people must have certain physical needs met to have a decent shot at happiness), but it is no guarantee. There are countries with abundant resources and little happiness. And there are countries near the top of the happiness report that have little in the way of natural resources.

Interestingly, I suspect right wing "American exceptionalists" will sneer at the idea that any country could rank higher in happiness than us. They should get out more. Meanwhile, some on the left will sneer at the U.S. for not being at the top. How ironic that they would look down their noses at the exceptionalists, but then criticize us for not being number one.

Is our high ranking on the UN happiness report a moral good? I believe it is. Aristotle considered happiness to be the ultimate good. Whether or not one agrees with him, it is certainly a significant good, and any country that has in place the conditions that make for happiness is surely providing a moral good. And when you can do that for a nation of 323 million people (considering that the 17 nations ranked ahead of us are much smaller and much more homogeneous—to again raise the issue of the elephant in the room addressed by Jonathan Haidt in the introduction), that is all the more reason to celebrate.

CHA**5**TER

Healthy, Smart, and Living Well

One UN study surveys the countries of the world for what is known as the human development index. This study is based on three criteria: health, education, and standard of living. In this index of 188 countries, the United States ranks tenth (tied with Canada).[50] The nine countries above us have a combined population that is less than half of ours. Some of the many countries ranked below us include New Zealand, Sweden, the UK, Japan, France, Belgium, Finland, Austria, Italy, and Spain. To be ranked above those countries suggests we are doing well, because those are all certainly good countries. Here I reiterate an argument I made in previous chapters. Those who insist that the U.S. is a systemically and oppressively racist nation in which people of color are held under the thumb of white people will have to rethink their position. Such a high ranking would be highly unlikely mathematically if a nation kept nearly 40 percent of its population living under the thumb of systemic and oppressive racism.

Even more impressive is where the U.S. ranks on the OECD Better Life Index.[51] The OECD is the Organization for Economic Co-operation and Development, founded in 1961. Their index takes eleven key factors of human well-being into consideration and ranks all of its thirty-five member-nations, plus three more. The eleven factors are housing, income, jobs, community, education, environment, civic engagement, health, life satisfaction, safety, and work/life balance. If you go to the site and click on "Display countries by rank," you will find that the U.S. ranks eighth of the thirty-eight countries ranked. We trail only Norway, Denmark, Australia, Sweden, Canada, Switzerland, and Iceland. The combined population of those countries is 28 percent of the population of the U.S. So again I ask, who is doing more good for the world?

Why would I consider eighth of thirty-eight countries to be more impressive than tenth of 188 countries? It is because the competition, on average, is much greater. All thirty-eight countries in the OECD Index were in the UN Index. They were generally the top countries in the UN Index. So to be eighth in the more comprehensive OECD Index (more comprehensive in the sense that it weighs eleven factors, not three) means the U.S. had to leapfrog two countries that are definitely good countries.

Is our high ranking on these indices a moral good? I believe it is. A nation that is among the world's very best in providing a high quality of living (for a large number of people) has surely accomplished something which must be regarded as morally good.

CHAPTER 6

Charity May Begin at Home, But It Should Not End There

Charity is a deceptively difficult topic to deal with. Let me begin with the UK-based Charities Aid Foundation's most recent report. In their study of nations around the world, they rank the charitable nature of nations according to three criteria: the willingness of a nation's people to help a stranger, donate money to a charity, and volunteer time to an organization.

The first thing you may notice when looking through the report is one glaring difference between this ranking and so many others (including those we have looked at in previous chapters). The rankings are not dominated by the developed nations of the world. The top three countries are Myanmar, Indonesia, and Kenya. The U.S. ranks a very admirable fifth.[52]

Limiting our purview to some of the wealthier nations of the world, the Philanthropy Roundtable has found the following giving levels by country (this is annual private philanthropy as a percentage of GDP):

1. U.S.	1.44 percent
2. Canada	0.77 percent
3. UK	0.54 percent
4. South Korea	0.50 percent
5. Singapore	0.39 percent
6. Italy	0.30 percent
6. (tie) Netherlands	0.30 percent
8. Australia	0.23 percent
9. Ireland	0.22 percent
10. Germany	0.17 percent
11. Sweden	0.16 percent
12. Japan	0.12 percent
13. France	0.11 percent
14. China	0.03 percent

The Philanthropy Roundtable then discusses other forms of aid:

A number of studies have been undertaken to compare the charitable giving of various countries in fair ways—adjusting for differences in standards of living, population, and so forth. All end up showing about the same relationship that is charted here: Americans are about twice as generous in their private giving as our kissing cousins the Canadians, and 3–15 *times* as charitable as the residents of other developed nations. Americans also volunteer more than almost any other wealthy people.

Another very large source of economic assistance to the overseas poor, which we have chosen not to depict here but which has been painstakingly estimated in the Hudson Institute report from which this data is taken, is remittances sent back home by U.S. immigrants from poor lands. These amount to over a hundred billion dollars every year, and are more important to family welfare, health, and education in many underdeveloped countries than either private or governmental charity.

Anyone trying to understand the financial flows that aid the poor overseas must also consider one final element: private investment in developing countries. More than $179 billion of U.S. capital was committed to projects in poor nations in 2014, with for-profit aspirations. This job- and growth-creating money is probably the most important form of all of international sharing.[53]

But there are many complications, and that is what makes this subject so difficult. To begin with, many of the developed countries have less poverty than ours and so people literally see less need. Of course, that wouldn't explain the amount of American giving that goes to poor nations. But yet another complication is that in many of the developed countries, the giving is done by the countries by way of the higher taxes people pay. Consider the following data from the OECD; the figures represent governmental development assistance to developing and other countries in need from the developed world as a percentage of gross national income:

1. Sweden	1.40 percent
2. Norway	1.05 percent
3. Luxembourg	0.93 percent
4. Denmark	0.85 percent
5. Netherlands	0.76 percent
6. United Kingdom	0.71 percent

7. Finland	0.56 percent
8. Switzerland	0.52 percent
9. Germany	0.52 percent
10. Belgium	0.42 percent
11. France	0.37 percent
12. Ireland	0.36 percent
13. Austria	0.32 percent
14. Canada	0.28 percent
15. New Zealand	0.27 percent
15. (tie) Australia	0.27 percent
17. Iceland	0.24 percent
18. Japan	0.22 percent
19. Italy	0.21 percent
20. United States	0.17 percent
21. Portugal	0.16 percent
22. Slovenia	0.15 percent
23. Greece	0.14 percent
23. (tie) South Korea	0.14percent
25. Spain	0.13 percent
26. Czech Republic	0.12 percent
27. Slovak Republic	0.10 percent
27. (tie) Poland	0.10 percent[54]

This table uses gross national income (GNI), while the previous table used gross domestic product (GDP). A quick Google search showed that for five countries I randomly checked (Sweden, France, Canada, the UK, and the U.S.), the difference between the two figures is not great (all figures in dollars). The GDP for the U.S. is $18.59 trillion, while its GNI is $18.75 trillion; the figures for the other countries are $511 billion and $495 billion (Sweden), $2.5 trillion and $2.8 trillion (France), $2.6 trillion and $2.8 trillion (the U.K.), and $1.5 trillion and $1.6 trillion (Canada).

There is a remarkable symmetry between the two countries at the top of the two charts, Sweden and the U.S. Private giving in the U.S. is 1.44 percent of GDP, while in Sweden it is 0.16 percent. But assistance by country for Sweden is 1.40 percent of GNI, while in the U.S. it is 0.17 percent.

Critics of the U.S. will note that 32 percent of private charitable giving in the U.S. goes to religious organizations. Few will doubt that these organizations do a lot of good, but there is also no doubt that much of what they take in goes to overhead (clergy salaries and building maintenance, for example). Of course, government giving is hardly free of overhead, either.

Furthermore, dwarfing the aid given by countries (by a factor of three-to-one) is the amount of money being sent home from migrants to their homelands. In a Daily Mail.com article, Simon Tomlinson reports on this so-called remittance money:

> The amount of money being sent by migrants across the entire world reached $530 billion last year, making it a larger economy than Iran or Argentina, the data from the World Bank showed.
>
> This worldwide figure has tripled in the last ten years and is now three times bigger than the total aid budgets given by countries around the world. It has sparked debate whether this so-called remittance money could be a viable alternative to relying on help from other governments.
>
> In the United States last year, more than $120 billion was sent by workers to families abroad—making it the largest sender of remittances in the world. More than $23 billion went to Mexico, $13.45 billion to China, $10.84 billion to India, and $10 billion to the Philippines, among other

recipients.[55] [Note: This raw figure given for the U.S. looks quite large, but when taken on a per capita basis we find that many developed countries actually have higher remittance figures. However, as we saw with immigration, a majority of the remittance giving of the other developed countries is giving among themselves. The overwhelming majority of U.S. remittance giving goes to poor countries. Furthermore, one must also take into account remittance inflow which is quite high in many developed countries – obviously, if they are spreading the money among themselves - but very low in the U.S. See The World Bank "Migration and Remittance Factbook 2016" for all the data you could ever want.]

And complicating all of the above, as if it's not complicated enough already, is the fact that the U.S. has spent monumental funds on defense. Of course, some would argue that that money has done more harm than good. I would disagree and I address that topic in chapter 16. But there is no denying that these funds have provided an umbrella of protection for the free world countries since the end of WWII. That has allowed these countries to spend more of their funds on assistance.

The bottom line is that comparing the charitable natures of countries is a terribly complicated matter. I certainly am not trying to suggest that the U.S. is the most generous nation on Earth, but taking all of the above data into account, and not forgetting that the chapter began with a fifth place world ranking for the U.S. from the Charities Aid Foundation, I believe the conclusion is inescapable that the U.S. is a very generous nation, wherever you choose to rank it (if, indeed, it even makes sense to rank such things). Is U.S. generosity a moral good? I certainly think so. It would be interesting to hear an argument that it is not.

CHAPTER 7

The Incredible Shrinking Middle Class

We hear much about the decline of the middle class in the U.S., and it is indeed true that it is shrinking. But the assumption many make is that people are falling out of the middle class into lower classes. That assumption is false. A 2016 report from the liberal Urban Institute tells an amazing story. The study looked at the period from 1979–2014. It broke down the American population into five income groups: the rich, the upper middle class, the middle class, the lower middle class, and the poor or near poor. The middle class did indeed shrink from 38.8 percent of the population to 32.0 percent. But the lower middle class also shrank, from 23.9 percent to 17.1 percent, as did the poor and near poor from 24.3 percent to 19.8 percent (and the latter figure is significantly and misleadingly high, as we will see in Chapter 11).

So where did all these middle-class Americans go? The rich rose from 0.1 percent of the population to 1.8 percent. But those percentages are far too small to account for many Americans. The answer is found in the upper middle class, which grew remarkably from 12.9 percent of the population to 29.4 percent.[56] So it turns out that, yes, the middle class is shrinking, but not so much because people are falling down but because they are rising up.

Is this development, which probably comes as a surprise to many, a moral good? I believe it is. It is a moral good when a nation sees significant material well-being for more and more people over a thirty-five-year period. I don't see any moral virtue in the increase in the number of rich, but I certainly do in the shrinking percentage of the lower middle class, and of the poor and near poor.

CHAPTER 8

A Remarkable Reinvention of Society

Asked to name the most pivotal movement or era in human history since the dawn of civilization, some might name the beginnings of organized religion, some might name the Islamic Golden Age, some might name the Renaissance, some might name the great empires of Central and South America, and some might name the glory of Greece and Rome. I would not name any of these. My selection is that period known as the Enlightenment. It directly led to the betterment of human beings around the globe in a manner no other movement can touch. Americans played a minor role in the beginning of this movement, but have played a crucial role in its continuing impact.

Beginning largely in the eighteenth century, the Enlightenment led to a profound reshaping of the structure of societies. Where hierarchies once held sway, with a few men (and they were almost always men) on top and the vast majority of the people beneath them, eighteenth century Enlightenment thinkers began to speak of such things as social equality and liberty. The remarkable result would be respect for commoners as people who mattered, people whose ideas were worth listening to, people with rights and free-doms. This did not all happen overnight, of course, and not for all people at once, but when one looks over the entire sweep of human history, and the glacial rate at which change over vast swaths of the world generally happens, the light lit by the Enlightenment spread like wildfire at a staggeringly improbable rate. This was the birth of what is often called classical liberalism, not to be con-fused with what we generally call liberalism today.

The Enlightenment was largely a British and French move-ment, and they deserve lavish praise for what they brought about. This fact requires that I ask you to indulge me for a number of pages as we cross the Atlantic to explore some of the seeds of the Enlightenment that eventually blossomed into much of what is good about this country. Pivotal figures included such well-known individuals as Voltaire, Jean-Jacques Rousseau, John Locke, Adam Smith, David Hume, and Mary Wollstonecraft. But I would like to bring in a lesser known figure, the Scottish clergyman Francis Hutcheson (1694–1746). Unlike nearly all thinkers before him, Hutcheson believed that all human beings are born with an innate moral sense. In *How the Scots Invented the Modern World*, historian Arthur Herman introduces us to the thinking of Hutcheson:

> In other words, we are born to make moral judgments, just as we are born with a mouth to eat and eyes to see. Moral reasoning is a natural human faculty, but it differs from other kinds of reasoning, such as judging distances or adding up columns of numbers. It is expressed through our feelings and emotions. The most important is love,

particularly love for others, which is the starting point of all morality. Love also proves that man is not inherently selfish, as Thomas Hobbes had claimed. 'There is no mortal,' Hutcheson asserted, 'without some love toward others, and desires in the happiness of some other persons as well as his own.' A benevolent 'fellow-feeling' for other creatures and a 'delight in the Good of others' becomes the basis of our sense of right and wrong. We decide that what helps and pleases a person we love is good, because it also gives us pleasure. What injures him is bad, because it causes us pain to see him unhappy. We begin to realize that the happiness is also our happiness.

Everyone's ultimate goal in life, Hutcheson decided, is happiness."It is the inner glow we feel when we make a child smile. For Hutcheson, our emotional lives reach out, instinctively, toward others, in bonds of affection and love, in ever-widening circles, as our interactions with others grow and become more numerous.

Self-interest and altruism are no longer at odds. In our highest moral state they merge and become 'two forces compelling the same body to motion.' They form 'an invariable constant impulse towards one's own perfection and happiness of the highest kind' and 'toward the happiness of others.' Virtue is indeed its own reward. But it is the highest reward of all—a contented mind and soul.

If three hundred years later, all this sounds ludicrously naïve, we need to think again. Hutcheson was no fool... He knew people could behave viciously and hurt others. He knew human beings often ignore their consciences and the 'bonds of beneficence and humanity' that bind us together in society.

But, he was asserting, that is not their true nature.[57]

Hutcheson was a religious man, but of a gentle sort. He "never lost sight of his main goal: 'to change the face of theology in Scotland,' as he put it. He wanted to turn his fellow clergymen away from the hard, inflexible dogmas of John Knox...Hutcheson wanted the Presbyterian faith to take on a more humane, comforting face." Hutcheson's main point was that "the message of Christianity was above all a moral message. The pulpit was not a place to inspire fear and terror, but to uplift and inspire."[58]

Interestingly, Hutcheson seems to have been prescient enough to pre-shadow modern thought on the evolution of humans as social beings. Modern thought on the evolution of morality has obviously moved well beyond Hutcheson's thinking, but he would be far more comfortable in a university class today on the origins of morality than would most of his contemporaries or predecessors.

His students at the University of Glasgow in the first half of the eighteenth century learned from Hutcheson that "the underlying principle of all human behavior were parts of an 'immense and connected' moral system governed by the dictates of natural law." Such natural law included "'private rights, or the laws obtaining in natural liberty.'

> The crucial element in each, the part that enabled everything else to move, was always the same: liberty...it applies to all human beings everywhere, regardless of origin or status.

> Hutcheson took this basic principle of liberty out beyond the political realm. He not only endorsed Lockean ideas of

freedom of speech and freedom of religion. He challenged other forms of oppression which Locke...had ignored.

One was the legal subjugation of women. Hutcheson defined rights as universal, and did not recognize any distinction based on gender. The other, even more important, was slavery. 'Nothing,' he said, 'can change a rational creature into a piece of goods void of all rights.' In fact, Hutcheson's lectures, published after his death...would inspire antislavery abolitionists, not only in Scotland but from London to Philadelphia.[59]

While I have used the thought of Hutcheson as an example of the revolutionary nature of Enlightenment thought, he was obviously just a part of a sea change in thought that over the course of the next two centuries would transform the world in unprecedented fashion. The Enlightenment would lead to the eradication of slavery, the movement for women's rights, the reform of prisons, freedom of speech and press and religion, and a way of thinking about economics that also stressed liberty and resulted in capitalism, a force that has enriched the world to a truly astonishing degree.

With regard to slavery, Walter Williams reminds us:

Slavery had been part of the human condition throughout recorded history and everywhere on the globe. Romans enslaved other Europeans; Greeks enslaved other Greeks; Asians enslaved Asians, Africans enslaved Africans; and in the New World Aztecs enslaved Aztecs and other native groups. Even the word slave is derived from the fact that Slavic people were among the early European slaves.

...A unique aspect of slavery in the Western World was the moral outrage against it, which began to emerge in

the eighteenth century and led to massive efforts to elimi-
nate it.[60]

A unique aspect of slavery in the U.S., and an interesting aside,
was the need to justify it. Many of those who founded this nation
were opposed to slavery and owned no slaves. Many did own
slaves but were deeply conflicted. They knew that their owner-
ship of slaves violated the principles on which the country was
founded. Like all of us who try to justify to ourselves behaviors
we know are wrong, they made up an excuse to assuage their consciences. That excuse, economist Thomas Sowell says, was racism.
Sowell makes the counterintuitive observation that it is slavery
that led to racism in the United States and not racism that led to
slavery. Noting that slavery was widespread around the world as
a fact of life not needing to be defended, he concludes that in the
U.S., the birth of our country in liberty made the institution of
slavery morally precarious and in need of a defense. And so it is
that racism became the defense. "Racism became a justification of
slavery in a society where it could not be justified otherwise—and
centuries of racism did not suddenly vanish with the abolition of
the slavery that gave rise to it. But the direction of causation was
the direct opposite of what is assumed by those who depict the
enslavement of Africans as being a result of racism."[61]

Apart from its social effects, the Enlightenment precipitated
enormous advances in greater material well-being. The libertarian
economist Deirdre McCloskey notes that for several thousands of
years prior to 1800, human beings lived on about $3 per day. There
were certain brief bump-ups in this figure (maybe rising as much
as 400 or 500 percent) during brief epochs, but soon the number
returned to that relatively stable baseline. The Enlightenment then
brought about what McCloskey calls "The Great Enrichment."

Economists and historians," McCloskey writes, "agree on its startling magnitude: By 2010, the average daily income in a wide range of countries...had soared 1,000 to 3,000 percent over the levels of 1800.

What then caused this Great Enrichment?

Not exploitation of the poor, not investment, not existing institutions, but a mere idea, which the philosopher and economist Adam Smith called 'the liberal plan of equality, liberty and justice.' In a word, it was liberalism, in the free-market European sense. Give masses of ordinary people equality before the law and equality of social dignity, and leave them alone, and it turns out that they become extraordinarily creative and energetic.

Since Karl Marx, we have made a habit of seeking material causes for human progress. But the modern world came from treating more and more people with respect.[62]

As Thomas Sowell has said, human beings began in poverty. It is not poverty, but prosperity, that needs explaining. This period of "enrichment," as McCloskey calls it, achieved more material progress in two hundred years than had been accomplished since the dawn of civilization.

The liberty that Enlightenment figures called for was not limited to such things as freedom of speech or the right to vote or the eradication of slavery. It also extended to the marketplace. McCloskey argues that for an innovative society, you have to have lots of people trying things out. The freedom to do so was new and was spawned by the equality of social standing Adam Smith (a student of Hutcheson) called for. This, McCloskey argues, gave the common person the right to "have a go at it." All ideas were on the table and the results transformed the world. The more countries that opt for free markets, the richer the world gets. And it has been getting richer, even in places normally thought of as desperately poor, such as Africa.

One piece of the liberty puzzle often overlooked is the right to own property. That piece of liberty was important to the Enlightenment figures. If what you have can be taken away by the whim of the state (or by individuals because the state doesn't protect you), you lose all incentive to innovate and create. The great Peruvian economist Hernando De Soto (described in 2004 by Bill Clinton as "probably the world's most important living economist") has perhaps done more than any economist to argue for the connection between property rights and prosperity. In 1950, the African nation of Botswana was the fourth poorest in the world. It seemed to have little hope for the future. Yet the future cannot always be read well. Matt Ridley tells us:

> But Botswana did not fail. It succeeded not just moderately well, but spectacularly. In the thirty years after independence it grew its per capita GDP faster on average (nearly 8 percent) than any other country in the entire world—faster than Japan, China, South Korea and America during that period. It multiplied its per capita income thirteen times so that its average citizens are now richer than Thais, Bulgarians, or Peruvians. It has had no coups, civil wars, or dictators. It has experienced no hyperinflation or debt default. It did not wipe out its elephants. It is consistently the most successful economy in the world in recent decades.

> It is true that Botswana has a small and ethnically somewhat homogeneous population [my note: there's that elephant in

the room again], unlike many other countries. But its biggest advantage is one that the rest of Africa could easily have shared: good institutions. In particular, Botswana turns out to have secure, enforceable property rights that are fairly widely distributed and fairly well respected. When [MIT economist] Daron Acemoglu and his colleagues compared property rights with economic growth throughout the world, they found that the first explained an astonishing three quarters of the variation in the second and that Botswana was no outlier: the reason it had flourished was because its people owned property without fear of confiscation by chiefs or thieves to a much greater extent than in the rest of Africa. This is much the same explanation for why England had a good eighteenth century while China did not.[63]

The afterglow of the Enlightenment has not dimmed. Those countries touched by it continue to find new ways to make their corners of the globe a better place, and in doing so, elevate the entire globe, if only by example.

And Enlightenment thought continues its relentless march at home. In 2016 *The Economist* reported, "As recently as 1964, even the American Civil Liberties Union agreed that homosexuals should be barred from government jobs. In 1987, only 48 percent of Americans approved of interracial dating; in 2012 that figure was 86 percent (and 95 percent of 18- to 29-year-olds)."[64]

The highly regarded Stanford University scientist Robert Sapolsky admits that his political instincts run to the left, and he says he sympathizes with those who feel the Enlightenment has been overvalued and fueled western neo-imperialism. But being the honest scientist that he is, he cannot help but add, "Nevertheless, one must admit that the countries with minimal violence, extensive social safety nets, few child brides, numerous female legislators, and sacrosanct civil liberties are usually direct cultural descendants of the Enlightenment."[65]

What has this historical era we call the Enlightenment to do with the United States, you might be wondering. There are two connections I wish to point out. The first is that while British and French thinkers led the Enlightenment, the fledgling United States, even in the colonial period before there was a United States, had a number of original Enlightenment thinkers greatly admired by the Europeans. These included Thomas Paine, Benjamin Franklin, Thomas Jefferson, and James Madison, among others. The second is that the moral and philosophical foundations that gave rise to our constitutional form of government are products of Enlightenment thought and proved to be an inspiration to many other countries in the decades and centuries that followed the founding of the United States. Many nations have built democratic republics on the U.S. model. These countries are not naïve. They realize that we struggled and still struggle to live up to the ideals we built on. But they must also realize that even when those ideas are only on paper, better to be on paper where they can light a fire under the feet of those in power than not be at all. That our nation has managed to play a role in the greatest movement in human history, and has been inspirational in extending that movement to others, is surely a moral good.

CHA**9**TER

Teach the Children Well, and Don't Stop at Childhood

Periodically, we are treated to newspaper articles bemoaning the state of education in the United States. This may be more a function of the reality that bad news sells more newspapers than it is a sober assessment of education in this country, but that is not to deny that there is troubling data out there. A 2017 Pew Research Study sums up its findings with these words: "Internationally, U.S. stands in middle of pack on science, math, reading scores." I find that statement a bit misleading. First, the article leads with the worst news, and in my opinion doesn't even get that very accurate. We read first about the cross-national test, PISA (Programme for International Student Assessment), which tests 15-year-olds. In math the U.S. placed thirty-eighth out of the seventy-one countries studied. That does sound like "middle of the pack" as the quote above suggests. But in both science and reading, the U.S.

45

placed twenty-fourth of seventy-one countries (and ahead of the average score of the OECD countries in each category). That's hardly "middle of the pack." That's virtually top third (twenty-four of seventy-two would be top third). "Middle of the pack" makes even less sense when we move on to the next cross-national test, the TIMSS (Trends in International Mathematics and Science Study). This is a study of students in grades four and eight. There the U.S. fourth-graders ranked eleventh of forty-eight countries in math and eighth of forty-eight in science. U.S. eighth-graders ranked eighth of thirty-seven countries in both math and science.[66] Middle of the pack?

A study out of the Stanford Graduate School of Education and the Economic Policy Institute, reported by Jonathan Rabinovits, suggests that comparing U.S. students to foreign students often yields misleading results because the socioeconomic inequality among U.S. students skews international comparison of test scores. When that difference is taken into account, say the authors of the study, Martin Carnoy and Richard Rothstein, "The gap between U.S. students and those from the highest achieving countries would be cut in half in reading and by at least a third in math."[67] The study also found that "Achievement of U.S. disadvantaged students has been rising rapidly over time, while achievement of disadvantaged students in countries to which the United States is frequently unfavorably compared – Canada, Finland, and Korea, for example – has been falling rapidly."[68] Furthermore, "U.S. PISA scores are depressed partly because of a sampling flaw resulting in a disproportionate number of students from high-poverty schools among the test takers. About 40 percent of the PISA sample in the United States was drawn from schools where half or more of the students are eligible for the free lunch program, though only 32 percent of students nationwide attend such schools."[69]

Some might say, "Well, shame on the United States for having more children from lower socioeconomic classes." Such an argument overlooks the fact, however, that racial and ethnic minorities overall do less well economically just about anywhere you look in the western world. It just happens that the U.S. has far more such people (not just in raw numbers, but as a percentage of the population – which is the significant figure). The Canadian Union of Public Employees reports that numbers from the 2016 census show that non-white Canadians have incomes about thirty percent less than white Canadians.[70] This is greater than the discrepancy in the U.S. Moving to the UK, Omar Khan of the Runnymede Trust, a British race equality think tank, writes that the racial wealth gap in the U.S. is not only an American problem (he is writing about accumulated wealth as opposed to annual income, though the two are intricately related).

> Ethnic minorities in the United Kingdom also lag behind white people in accumulating wealth, and this is probably true across Europe. This disparity is bad for everyone.

> In the UK, the government has collected data on ethnicity since the 1991 Census, and public authorities are required to monitor ethnicity. In contrast, in most European countries collecting data on ethnicity is *illegal*. We cannot precisely quantify wealth holdings elsewhere in European countries, but, by extrapolating from UK data and for reasons set forth below, we know that European ethnic minorities have fewer assets than white people on the continent.

> The UK's Department of Work and Pensions has found that 60 percent of black and Asian households have no savings at all, compared to 33 percent of white households.

The UK's first Wealth and Assets Survey in 2009 reported that while the average white household had £221,000 (roughly $350,000) in assets, Black Caribbean households had £76,000, Bangladeshi households £21,000 and Black African households £15,000.

There are a few explanations for these low levels of asset-holding. First is that ethnic minorities and migrants in the UK – and indeed in Europe – are more likely to earn low incomes. As any visitor to London, Brussels, Paris or Rome will know, African, Asian and East European migrants do many of the low-paid, low-security jobs that don't provide access to many European benefits, and that makes it difficult to save.[71]

Try doubling, tripling, quadrupling, or quintupling the number of racial and ethnic minorities European countries have (so that they approach the reality in the U.S.; you will have to multiply by a different number depending on which country you are talking about) and then see what happens to test scores (remembering the correlation Carnoy and Rothstein found between economic disadvantage and test scores).

Returning to the study on comparison of students across countries by Carnoy and Rothstein, we find out that supposedly objective testing can be a very subjective thing. Rabinovits writes:

Carnoy and Rothstein say that the differences in average scores on these tests reflect arbitrary decisions about content by the designers of the tests. For example, although it has been widely reported that U.S. 15-year-olds perform worse on average than students in Finland in mathematics, U.S. students perform better than students in Finland in algebra but worse in number properties (e.g., fractions). If algebra had greater weight in tests, and numbers less weight, test scores could show that U.S. overall performance was superior to that of Finland.[72]

Finally, U.S. taxpayers are quite generous when it comes to supporting schools. According to the World Economic Forum, the U.S. ranks in a tie for fifth among OECD nations in educational spending as a percentage of GDP.[73] Nor is all that money being spent on white students. A liberal UCLA law professor, Richard Sander, and a liberal Los Angeles legal journalist, Stuart Taylor Jr., studied school spending in the United States and found that, "There is some debate whether the nation's per capita education spending on blacks is higher or lower than its spending on whites, but there is no debate that the levels are close."[74] That said, it may well be that after years of neglect we may have to spend considerably more on the education of students from lower socioeconomic classes.

At the end of the day, I am left to conclude that even with significant room for improvement, the United States provides a level of education in grade school and high school that is a moral good. I don't think the conclusion is overwhelming, but I think it is fair and reasonable.

What can be said with a high degree of certainty is that when it comes to university excellence the U.S. is at the top of the heap. The Center for World University Rankings (CWUR) publishes the only global university ranking that measures the quality of education and training of students, as well as the prestige of the faculty members and the quality of their research without relying on surveys and university data submissions. Of the top twenty-five universities in their global ranking, nineteen are U.S. institutions (as well as thirty-two of the top fifty).[75] The ranking done by the British-based *Times Higher Education* gives eighteen of the top twenty-five spots to U.S. institutions (as well as twenty-six of the top fifty).[76] These institutions have been a source of intellectual nourishment not only for Americans, but for people all over the world. They have inspired tremendous advances in nearly any field of study you can imagine. And they have produced for the world ideas most of us couldn't have imagined. One can safely say, I believe, that this tips the educational balance even further to the side of the moral good.

10

From the Dirt Beneath Us
to the Skies Above Us

When one thinks of scientific and technological developments brought to the world by the United States, one thinks of everything from mass-produced automobiles to the internet and the smartphone. In this chapter I would like to focus on some very divergent and less well-known developments that have saved countless lives and may someday save the planet.

One of the most unsung heroes in the history of humankind is a U.S. scientist by the name of Dr. Norman Borlaug. It would be difficult to come up with another single scientist who has done so much good for so many people in the world. In the mid-twentieth century, he developed semi-dwarf, high yield, disease resistant wheat varieties. These techniques were introduced first in the nations of Mexico, Pakistan, and India and later throughout the continents of Asia and Africa. He has been credited with saving up to one billion (that's not a typo—that's one "billion" with a "b") people from starvation. "Because of his achievements to prevent hunger, famine, and misery around the world, it is said that Dr. Borlaug has 'saved more lives than any other person who has ever lived.'"[77] Some would dispute that and claim the title for the German scientist, Fritz Haber, who developed modern pesticides. Fair enough. If I were writing this book about Germany I would certainly highlight Haber.

Moving away from agriculture, many of us are vaguely aware that the U.S. space program has spun off a number of benefits in seemingly unrelated areas, but until I Googled the topic I was unaware of the wide-ranging diversity of these benefits. Here is just a small sampling of technologies that have been improved by NASA spin-offs: artificial limbs, de-icing systems for aircraft, radial tires, land mine removal equipment, water purification systems, and heart pumps.

Critics might say that we could have developed those technologies without all the expense of the space program. To say that, though, is to reveal a deep misunderstanding of how progress often comes about. The spin-offs came about as the result of engineers trying to solve unique problems brought about by the space program. Only later were the applications to other areas realized. Necessity often is the mother of invention.

My particular interest here, though, is not the exploration of space for the historical reason most normally thought of (beating the Soviets to the moon), but rather the ongoing effort to protect humanity from a potential disaster of enormous proportions. I am referring to the threat to Earth from asteroids in our solar system. It is the U.S. that is leading the way in protecting Earth from such a catastrophe. The program is in its infancy, but one must start somewhere.

From NASA's Jet Propulsion Laboratory comes this sobering observation:

The famous meteor crater in northern Arizona, some 1,219 meters (4,000 feet) in diameter and 183 meters (600 feet) deep, was created 50,000 years ago by a nickel-iron meteorite perhaps 60 meters in diameter. It probably survived nearly intact until impact, at which time it was pulverized and largely vaporized as its $6-7 \times 10^{16}$ joules of kinetic energy were rapidly dissipated in an explosion equivalent to some 15 million tons of TNT! Falls of this class occur once or twice every 1,000 years...

It's too late for the dinosaurs, but today astronomers are conducting ever-increasing searches to identify all of the larger objects which pose an impact danger to Earth.[78]

What can humans do to protect themselves? Phil Plait is an astronomer who writes the Bad Astronomy blog for the online magazine, *Slate*. In 2014 he wrote:

If we want to prevent asteroid impacts from happening, the first thing we need to do is spot these threats. And we're working pretty hard on that...

As things stand now, we don't have the capability to find them all. But we will, soon. The huge Pan-STARRS telescope is looking deep for threats and is already producing data. LSST is a planned monster 8-meter telescope specifically designated to look for near-Earth objects and is expected to catalogue hundreds of thousands of them.

To extend our vision, two spacecraft are currently in the works, too...[79]

The large majority of these efforts are funded by the U.S. and the scientists involved come largely from the U.S. Of course, finding such threats is one thing. Doing something about them is another. B612 is a California-based non-governmental agency working on that very issue.[80] The group is led almost entirely by U.S.-trained and U.S.-based scientists and engineers.

Whether or not our efforts, along with those of other nations, will save lives in the future cannot be known. But what is known with certainty is that lives have already been saved by weather satellite technology.

The world's first successful weather satellite, TIROS-1, went into orbit on April 1, 1960 (the Vanguard sent up the year before was not considered a success). It was a primitive satellite, of course, but it launched an era that would allow humans around the world to have sufficient warning of dangerous weather to be able to take to safety. Although it was operational for just seventy-eight days, "This satellite forever changed weather forecasting," said Jane Lubchenco, undersecretary of commerce for oceans and atmosphere and National Oceanic and Atmospheric Administration (NOAA) administrator. "Since TIROS-1, meteorologists have far greater information about severe weather and can issue more accurate forecasts and warnings that save lives and protect property."[81]

Satellites do more than monitor weather. They are also used in the detection and monitoring of fires and snowfields. In remote areas of the world, they can sometimes alert authorities to a raging fire weeks before the fire might otherwise be noticed. They can detect fires smoldering underground before they can even be seen from the ground. They aid in tracking malaria risk by monitoring vegetation in malaria-prone areas. They can spot solar activity that could create problems for power grids. They are involved in searching for and finding people lost in places around the globe. They aid farmers with information about soil moisture, plant health, vegetation heights, and water supplies.[82]

Many nations now work jointly in "covering the globe," but the U.S. introduced the world to such technology in 1960 (the first Russian weather satellite went up in 1969, and the first western European satellite went up in 1977), and progress continues. *Scientific American* reported in its October 1, 2016 issue that:

> The U.S. National Oceanic and Atmospheric Administration and NASA plan to launch the first of four satellites that should deliver what the agencies call 'game-changing' capabilities for predicting both ordinary weather and dangerous storms such as hurricanes. These next-generation spacecraft are needed to replace the existing weather satellites, one of which reaches the end of its operational lifetime this year...
>
> The updated satellite will also feature an instrument that represents the first of its kind in orbit: a lightning mapper. This high-speed, near-infrared camera will detect lightning flashes over North and South America as well as the surrounding oceans, enabling forecasters to issue earlier warnings for severe storms. There are also onboard instruments to watch the sun and detect dangerous solar storms that can hurl charged electromagnetic particles at Earth. Better space weather forecasting could provide notifications of potential disruptions to power grids and satellite fleets.[83]

There is no way to tell how many lives have been saved by satellite technology. And we can only estimate the number of lives saved by other scientific advances. But from a single scientist pondering the dirt beneath his feet to scientists looking skyward to the heavens, the gains for humanity are incalculable. This surely is a moral good.

11

The Challenge of Lifting All Boats

In the process of becoming one of the world's wealthiest countries, the U.S. has seen many, but not all, of its citizens prosper. It is not my aim here to try to officiate the debate between economists who say that the government needs to do more and economists who say that the government needs to get out of the way. I am not qualified to even make that attempt. I could fill many pages with the problems we face as a nation dealing with poverty levels that we are often too squeamish to confront. But here I will focus on how much progress has been made. This is progress often ignored by the left and often used by the right as a reason to rest on our laurels.

The chapter on the shrinking middle class already alluded to this topic, as did the chapter on the UN Human Development Index, where the U.S. ranked tenth in the world in a ranking where living standard was one of the three criteria at play. Less directly, the chapter on our high ranking in the UN World Happiness Index and the chapter on where people would choose to migrate (would people want to come here if they didn't think they could make a good living?) also alluded to this topic.

One of the most viewed graphs in studies of poverty shows the percentage of Americans living in poverty from the year 1959 to the present (or at least a year as close to the present for which we have data; as I write this chapter in early 2018, the most recent year for which we have such data is 2016). This graph is often seen in part because it is visually stunning. The percentage of Americans living in poverty in 1959 was 22.4 percent. By 1969, just ten years later, that figure was 12.1 percent. This makes the left side of the graph look like a water slide. Sadly, that downward trend seems to end abruptly. As Christopher Jencks writes, with regard to this graph, in the *New York Review of Books*, "There was no clear trend in poverty after 1969, either up or down. The official rate rose in the wake of recessions, reaching 15 percent in 1983, 1993 and 2010–2012, and it fell during recoveries, dropping to 11 or 12 percent in 1973, 1979, 2000, and 2006."[84]

Jencks, however, believes that the graph is misleading. In a remarkable bit of convergence, two divergent thinkers, Jencks from the left of center and Tim Worstall from the right of center, come to remarkably close conclusions as to what the real poverty rate is. Both, writing in 2015, use 2013 data when the poverty rate, according to the U.S. Census Bureau, was 14.5 percent (in 2016 the rate was 12.7 percent). Both come to the conclusion that the real rate in 2013 was below 5 percent (Worstall puts it at 4.5 percent, although elsewhere in his article he puts it at 4.8 percent, and Jencks puts it at 4.8 percent).

Why this discrepancy between the U.S. Census Bureau data and the figures Worstall and Jencks arrive at? Worstall gives us a rather succinct summary. He writes:

Welfare, poverty alleviation, in the U.S. in the 1960s was pretty much all about cash transfers. The U.S. system counts this as income in determining who is above or below the poverty line. Poverty alleviation today involves almost no cash transfers at all. Just about everything is done either through the tax system or transfers of goods and services. These are not counted as income when calculating who is above or below the poverty line.

Thus those '60s measures of poverty are the people who were still below the poverty line *after* poverty alleviation attempts [emphasis mine]. Today's numbers are, not exactly but to a sufficient level of accuracy, those who are below the poverty line *before* poverty alleviation attempts [emphasis mine].[85]

When Worstall adjusts for these factors, he gets a poverty rate in 2013 of 4.5 percent. It's a little confusing, as I mentioned above, because at one place in the article (including in the headline) he writes 4.5 percent, but at another place he gives us 4.8 percent. One wonders what the true rate would be for 2016 when the "published" rate was 12.7 percent. If the "real" rate (using 4.8 percent) fell at the same rate as the "published" rate, the poverty level in 2016 would have been 4.2 percent.

Jencks, in a much longer article, provides more detail on the nature of poverty alleviation methods used today, before arriving at the 4.8 percent figure. He also adds this interesting scenario not mentioned by Worstall:

Imagine two twenty-five-year-olds who are romantically involved, live together, and each earned $12,000 in 2013. If they were unmarried, the Census Bureau would have classified them as unrelated individuals, with poverty thresholds of $12,119 each. Since their incomes were only $12,000, the bureau would have counted them both as poor. They would each have needed at least $12,199...for the bureau to stop counting either of them as poor.

Had they been married, however, the bureau would have taken a more upbeat view of their economic situation, classifying them as a family of two with a poverty threshold of $15,600. As a result of this change, they would have both been above their poverty threshold instead of below it. According to the Census Bureau's most recent data, 11 percent of all opposite-sex couples who lived together in 2012 were unmarried [my note: he doesn't address how much higher the figure would be if we included same-sex couples]. We don't have such a figure for 1964, but it was probably only 1 or 2 percent. The assumption that cohabiting couples need more income than married couples has therefore raised the official poverty rate...The Census Bureau has never tried to defend the assumption, presumably because it is a byproduct of rules set by the Office of Management and Budget, which the Census must follow whether it likes them or not.[86]

Interestingly, both conservatives and liberals aren't particularly happy with what is really good news. Conservatives don't want to admit that government programs have helped to alleviate poverty, and liberals don't want to give up their talking point that conservatives are waging war upon the poor, a talking point that loses more and more steam as the number of poor dwindle.

While they argue that out, we should be able to agree that even though there is still work to be done, the decreasing number of poor in this country is a moral good.

12

Satisfaction with Life

I have to admit that the results of a Gallup Poll taken between June 7 and July 1, 2016, surprised me (pleasantly). Gallup asked the following question of Americans:

> Overall, how satisfied are you with your life? Are you very satisfied, somewhat satisfied, somewhat dissatisfied, or very dissatisfied?

Among whites, 89 percent considered themselves as somewhat satisfied or very satisfied. Among blacks, the figure was 88 percent, and among Hispanics it was 85 percent. Note that the date of the poll takes in a significant block of the black experience since Ferguson. A critic might think that since the poll lumps "very satisfied" and "somewhat satisfied" together, a breakdown of the two categories might show that whites lean much more toward "very satisfied" and blacks and Hispanics lean much more toward "somewhat satisfied." The critic would be wrong. If you go to the Gallup Poll, near the bottom you have the opportunity to look inside the numbers and you will find fairly even splits. For whites it's 47/42, for blacks it's 44/44, and for Hispanics it's 43/42. As for those who were "somewhat dissatisfied" or "very dissatisfied," the results are nearly the same: for whites, 8 percent and 2 percent, for blacks, 8 percent and 3 percent, and for Hispanics, 9 percent and 3 percent. Gallup also polled people on how satisfied they were with the direction in which the country is going, and blacks and Hispanics were about 75 percent more satisfied than whites.[87]

Such high levels of satisfaction with life, and optimism about the future, critically weaken the case of those who think this country is largely a land of white privilege in which people of color live under systemic and oppressive rule. There was a time, of course, when that was the case. The fact that we have moved so far away from that is, I believe, an unquestionable moral good.

CHAPTER **13**

Melting Pot or Salad Bowl?

For a long time the U.S. has been referred to as a "melting pot." The metaphor suggests that when people came to the U.S. they assimilated themselves into the culture of this country. Poles, Jews, Germans, Chinese, and countless others were willing to leave behind some of their own traditional ways to adopt the customs of their new land. But they didn't have to leave everything behind, so the so-called melting pot did not do away with everything that came to us from distant shores.

Modern multicultural thought has questioned the melting pot metaphor as putting too much emphasis on assimilation. The preferred alternative is to think in terms of a salad bowl, in which different cultures mix while still maintaining their cultural uniqueness.

But why, I wonder, must this be an either/or situation? In reality, hasn't it always been more of a both/and situation (how else to explain things like Chinatowns, St. Patrick's Day, and our eclectic mix of music, food, and literature)?

One area in which the melting pot metaphor has worked especially well is that of the assimilation of very different religious groups. Most recently, we have seen that happening among the 3.4 million Muslims in this country. *Boston Globe* columnist Jeff Jacoby, citing a Pew Research Center study, wrote about them in 2017:

> U.S. Muslims are replicating the age-old trajectory of religious minority communities: They adopt American values, reject fundamentalism, and form ties of friendship and love across religious lines.
>
> In the latest poll, an overwhelming 92 percent of Muslims agree with the patriotic statement, 'I am proud to be an American.' When asked how much they feel they have in common with most Americans, 60 percent of Muslims say 'a lot' and another 28 percent say 'some.' Only 36 percent say that all or most of their friends are fellow Muslims, a striking drop from the 49 percent who said so in the 2011 survey—and far less than the 95 percent of Muslims who say so in other countries…
>
> As the Pew data show, the Muslim community in America is the most religiously tolerant and socially liberal Islamic population in the world. And Muslims in America, far from sanctioning deliberate violence against civilians, are actually more likely than the general public to oppose it in all circumstances.[88]

So how do we make sense of these findings with the growing concern for Islamophobia in the U.S.? Perhaps the answer is that the concern is overblown. That is not to suggest that there is no animus among non-Muslims in the U.S. toward Muslims. But actual incidents of religious hate crimes are far more rare than many assume. In fact, Muslims are not even the ones most likely to be victimized by such crimes. They trail the Jews and have for as far back as you would probably care to look. This was true even in 2002, the first full year following 9/11.

According to the FBI, in 2016 there were 862 Jewish victims and 388 Muslim victims of religious hate crimes.[89] Of course, we must take into account the populations of the two groups (in 2016 there were 5.3 million Jews in the U.S. and 3.4 million Muslims). So crunching the numbers gives you the following: Jews are victims of religious hate crimes at the rate of 16.3 per 100,000 individuals, while Muslims are victims at the rate of 11.4 per 100,000. For some perspective, when you look at racial hate crimes (from the same FBI data used above) you find that blacks are victims at the rate of 5.2 per 100,000 and Hispanic or Latinos are victims at the rate of 0.9 per 100,000. When you look at sexual orientation hate crimes, you find that the LGBTQ community is victimized at the rate of 12.3 per 100,000. It should be noted that the FBI defines a hate crime as follows:

> A hate crime is a traditional offense like murder, arson, or vandalism with an added element of bias. For the purposes of collecting statistics, the FBI has defined a hate crime as a 'criminal offense against a person or property motivated in whole or in part by an offender's bias against a race, religion, disability, sexual orientation, ethnicity, gender, or gender identity.' Hate itself is not a crime—and the FBI is mindful of protecting freedom of speech and other civil liberties.[90]

For further perspective, it is worth our time to compare hate crimes in the U.S. with some other countries. Canada reported 221 hate crimes against Jews in 2016. With only 400,000 Jews in the country, that yields a rate of 55 per 100,000. Muslims were victims of 139 hate crimes in Canada, yielding a rate of 13.2 per 100,000. Blacks were victims of 214 hate crimes, yielding a rate of 17.8 per 100,000. The LGBTQ community were victims of 176 hate crimes, yielding a rate of 9.8 per 100,000.[91] Canada had fewer hate crimes against the LGBTQ community than the U.S., but more against blacks, Muslims, and Jews. The Canadian definition of a hate crime sounds much like the definition used in the U.S. Mark Freiman, a Canadian lawyer and former attorney general, tried to untangle the complicated nature of hate crime law in Canada in a March 1, 2017, piece on Canadian Television News:

> Freiman, who…prosecuted a case against Holocaust-denier Ernst Zundel, says that what many people refer to as 'hate crimes' are cases where judges have taken a guilty person's hateful motivations into account during sentencing.
>
> The Criminal Code includes guidance that says sentences shall take into account evidence 'that the offence was motivated by bias, prejudice, or hate based on race, national, or ethnic origin, language, colour, religion, sex, age, mental or physical disability, sexual orientation, or any other similar factor.'
>
> Complicating things further, police may or may not record that incident as a 'hate crime' in their statistics, depending on their own policies, which vary across the country.

As a result, holding up a sign outside of a mosque call-
ing for a ban on Muslim immigration would 'probably not
qualify' as public incitement of hate, Freiman said. Neither
would a single racial epithet yelled at a person walking
down the street.

For speech to qualify as inciting hate involves 'portraying the
subject of one's speech as being devoid of any positive qualities, demonization, dehumanization,' according to Freiman.[92]

Turning to the UK, we run into a difficulty. They often lump
together hate crimes and what they call "incidents." So they speak
of "hate crimes and incidents," although even that terminology
is not used consistently. This can make their numbers look much
worse compared to the U.S. and Canada. And yet looking through
the data, one can draw some fair conclusions. In 2016, there were
1,342 incidents against Jews in the UK according to a report in
the *Independent*. In a nation with only 270,000 Jews, that would
yield 497 offences per 100,000. But the same report indicates that
there were 108 violent assaults against Jews in 2016.[93] If we use
the number 108, we arrive at a figure of 40.0 per 100,000. That's
above the U.S. figure of 16.3 and below the Canadian figure of 55,
but clearly both the U.S. and Canada are including much more
than just "violent assaults" as hate crimes.

The bottom line is that anti-Semitism is a significantly greater
problem in the UK than in either Canada or the U.S. In fact,
when I Googled "anti-Semitic hate crimes in the UK," two of
the first twenty articles that appeared reported that many Jews
(as many as one-third of them) are considering leaving the UK. I
did the same search for Canada and the U.S., and in going fifty
articles deep I found no reports of Jews wanting to leave.

Moving to continental Europe, the situation remains grim and, in some places, worse. The internet is awash with articles from very respectable journals reporting on the growing anti-Semitism in the large countries of France and Germany, as well as in many smaller countries. In an in-depth article on the problem of anti-Semitism in France, there is a discussion of French Jews who seek to emigrate. We read the following: "Many others emigrate from France to the United Kingdom, where anti-Jewish racism is perceived as being a problem but less violent and severe than in France and to Canada and the United States, where the situation for Jews is all together different than in France; far safer and characterized by greater freedom and a general sense of security."[94] In Germany, the figure for violent attacks alone is 30.8 per 100,000, and in Sweden it is 53.3 per 100,000.[95] Interestingly, the figure for France is 21.3,[96] lower than Germany, Sweden, and the UK, and yet French Jews seem to feel more endangered than their counterparts in the UK. In any event, it is important to remember that all these European figures are for violent attacks only, while the U.S. figure of 16.3 per 100,000 is for all anti-Semitic hate crimes. It should be noted that some argue that the FBI data for the U.S. significantly underreports the true number of hate crimes. That may be true, but it would be naïve to think that other countries aren't prone to the same underreporting. In any event, it is little wonder that a Jewish professor once told my class that the United States is one of the best things to ever happen to the Jews. Judging by the Pew report on Muslim assimilation, I suspect there are many Muslims who would say the same.

For another way of looking at the "melting pot" issue, I turn to the author Bruce Bawer. When he wrote *Stealing Jesus: How Fundamentalism Betrays Christianity* in 1997, he became a darling of the left and the right hated him. When he wrote *While*

Europe Slept: How Radical Islam Is Destroying the West From Within in 2006, he became a darling of the right and the left now hated him. Interestingly, he wrote each book while living in the culture of which he spoke. Bawer grew up in the United States and wrote *Stealing Jesus* while still in the U.S. Shortly after that book came out he moved to Europe, first to the Netherlands (briefly) and then to Norway, where he still lives. Before bringing in his thoughts on the "melting pot," I need to share a bit of his story, which took him in his early forties from the U.S. to Western Europe.

When he first contemplated leaving New York City, he was thinking of moving elsewhere in the U.S. He has an abiding sense of love for this country. "The United States is not yet a perfect union (I've made a career out of lamenting its imperfections), but over the generations, it's gradually become better, fairer, more just—and it's done so by constantly struggling to be truer to its founding principles."[97] In time, though, he came to think that the best way to understand his native land was to live somewhere else. Having long admired Europe, he headed to Amsterdam first, a place he quickly appreciated.

> Yet as my weeks in the Old World stretched into months, my perceptions shifted. For one thing, I began to appreciate American virtues I'd always taken for granted, or even disdained—among them a lack of self-seriousness, an openness to new experience, an innate optimism, a willingness to think for oneself and question the accepted way of doing things…Europeans might or might not have more of a 'sense of history' than Americans (in fact, in a recent study comparing students' historical knowledge, the results were pretty much a draw), but America, I saw, had something else that mattered—a belief in the future.

Yes, many Europeans were book lovers—but which country's foreign literature engaged them most? America's. They revered education—but to which country's universities would they most like to send their children if they had the means? Answer: the same country that performs the majority of the world's scientific research, wins most of the Nobel Prizes, and has twice as many university graduates as Europe...

But the longer I stayed in Europe, the more I found myself viewing American ambition as a good thing. Life without it, I saw, could be a pretty pallid, hollow affair. Furthermore, I'd begun to see that in much of Western Europe, the appreciation of everyday pleasures was bound up with stifling conformity, a discomfort with excellence, and an overt disapproval of those who strove too visibly to better their lot. Sometimes it could even seem as if Western Europe's core belief was in mediocrity.

As I sought to ease my way into Dutch society, I felt the Dutch pushing back. I learned that if America was a melting pot...however long I might stay in the Netherlands...I would always remain an outsider.

I'd loved the peaceableness of Dutch men as compared to the macho swaggering of Americans. But the flip side of that un-macho behavior was a kind of passivity that, in the aftermath of 9/11, would emerge as something less than a perfect virtue.[98]

Moving to Norway in 1999, Bawer continued to see beneath the surface of what the left often portrays as heaven on Earth.

He admits to not knowing a lot about Norway when he first moved there.

> What I did know was that a staggering percentage of Norwegians bought three or more papers a day. I was awed. How different they were from Americans! How curious about the world! How well informed! In time, however, this enthusiasm was tempered. I saw that although Oslo had several daily papers, there was plenty of important news that somehow seemed never to be reported in any of them, and a wide range of opinion that virtually never made it anywhere near their editorial pages. By American standards, indeed, the papers' cumulative ideological range was quite narrow—from one end of the left to the other. The same went for the TV news operations, the largest being the government-owned NRK.[99]

Bawer also began to see that the "enlightened" Norwegians, and Scandinavians in general, who had prided themselves for so long on being free of the racism that plagued the United States, suddenly felt the sting of accusations of racism when their lily-white nations first experienced significant immigration of people of color at the end of the twentieth century and beginning of the twenty-first century. As Bawer notes, "Suddenly, their smug certainties were gone." All they could do was smother their misgivings.

This brings us back to the subject of immigration and assimilation.

> Comparing America's success with immigration and Europe's failure, she [Unni Wikan, a professor of social anthropology at the University of Oslo] explains that the

difference boils down to American realism versus European naivete. The pillars of U.S. immigration policy are integration and employment; officials in Western Europe, by contrast, thought they were doing immigrants a favor by not requiring—or even encouraging—either. One might wonder why European authorities didn't try to learn from the spectacularly successful history of U.S. immigration. I've lived in Europe long enough to know why: they didn't *see* it as a success story. In the eyes of the Western European establishment, America is a fundamentally racist and materialistic nation that cruelly compels immigrants to shake off their identities and fend for themselves under a heartless, dog-eat-dog economic system...

While immigrants in America are encouraged to become full members of society—and are rewarded for doing so—in Europe...the establishment prefers its immigrants unintegrated. Why? The supposed reason is that it respects differences, the real reason, as I gradually came to understand, was a profound discomfort with the idea of 'them' becoming 'us.' Immigrants in Europe are allowed to perpetuate even the most atrocious aspects of their culture, but the price for this is that no one, including themselves, will ever think of them as Dutch or German or Swedish. Most Americans, I think, would be shocked to realize how far short of America Europe falls in this regard.

Indeed, it's not going too far to say that there's a species of bigotry, widespread in Europe, that trumps anything you can easily find in the United States...[100]

At the end of the day, there seems to be no doubt that the U.S. is one country in which both the melting pot and salad bowl metaphors are apt. The ability of American immigrants over the generations to come to this land and to fit in with their fellow Americans (not always without growing pains, of course) is a moral good.

CHAPTER

14

Health Care in the United States

The health care system in the United States often comes under severe criticism, some of it justified (especially when health care and the poor is the topic). Often, though, many criticisms are accepted uncritically and people are led to believe that life is inevitably better under a government-run single-payer system. Many who take it as a given that the poor fare better under such a system might be surprised to know that a study of the U.S. and Canadian health-care systems, done by former director of the Congressional Budget Office June O'Neill (now with the free market-oriented American Enterprise Institute), "found that the relationship between income and health is greater in Canada than the United States."[101] And from a Canadian, Brian Crowley, who believes that his country's health care system is superior in many ways to that of the U.S., we hear that there is a problem with not having to pay for medical care (of course, Canadians do pay, but it is through taxes that are unseen when you go to the doctor). Crowley, managing director of the Macdonald-Laurier Institute, a national public policy think tank in Canada, points out that if you don't have to pay, it also means you're not a customer, and that negatively affects how you are treated. He wrote:

> One of the most important lessons I have learned from my contact with the Canadian Medicare system is that payment makes you powerful. And its absence makes you risible if not invisible.

> Now the articulate and the middle class do not let little things like that get them down. Even though they do not pay, they still get in the faces of the people providing service and make their wishes known. But often the vulnerable, the poor, the ill-educated, and the inarticulate are the ones who suffer the most because no one's well-being within the health care system depends on patients/consumers being well looked after. And by depriving them of the power of payment within the health care system, Medicare disempowers them. And the poor see this, because while they may be poor, they are not stupid.

> …Those most satisfied with their health care were not the least educated, but the best educated—those with postgraduate degrees.

> These findings are consistent with my view that Canada's system does, in fact, create multi-tiered health care where health care services are distributed on the basis of middle-class networks and ability to communicate one's needs aggressively to professional caregivers. It is the poor, the

vulnerable (including, most obviously, the sick) and the inarticulate who receive the worst care, because they cannot circumvent the system the way the middle class and its advocates can."[102]

It would be naïve, I think, to assume that Canada is an outlier and that in other nationalized health care systems the poor do as well as the wealthy. While I will point out later why infant mortality rates are useless in comparing health systems between countries, they can tell us something (not everything) about the relationship between income and health within a country. Among the poorer people in the UK are Caribbean blacks and Pakistani Asians. The wealthiest people in the UK are generally white. The infant mortality rates (the number of deaths per 1,000 live births) for Caribbean blacks and Pakistani Asians (2008 data) were 9.8 and 9.6 respectively. For British whites the figure was 4.5, and for other whites in the UK the figure was 4.3.[103] I asked Bruce Bawer, "Do you find that the poor in Norway (and elsewhere in Europe) really receive the same care as everyone else, or is that just the party line?" This is not like asking someone off the street to give me their opinion. Bawer is a cultural critic who makes it his business to watch for such things. He responded, "Repeatedly, I have observed that the well-off and connected here get a whole different level of care than people who are perceived as expendable."[104] Bawer's observations in Europe seem to mirror Crowley's in Canada. Providing health care for the poor is not a problem magically solved by having a nationalized health care system. It remains a difficult problem for all of us.

Much of the criticism of the U.S. health care system is based on erroneous notions of what a health care system is responsible for. Furthermore, that criticism usually fails to be balanced by considering the many good features of our health care system. It is those good features that will be highlighted in this chapter. Does our health care system have to be perfect in order for us to see it as a moral good? I don't think so (a good thing, because it is far from perfect), any more than every single person in the United States has to be happy for us to see our high level of national happiness as a moral good (Chapter 4), or any more than our educational system has to be perfect for us to be able to see it as a moral good (Chapter 9).

There will be a great deal of detail about the U.S. health system in what follows in this chapter, with my primary source being the research of Scott Atlas, formerly a professor of medicine at the Stanford University Medical Center and now a fellow at Stanford's Hoover Institute, a leading conservative think tank. But before going into that detail, it would be worth our time to consider two above-mentioned indices (in Chapter 5), which indicate that there is plenty right with U.S. medical care. In the UN Human Development Index (in which health was one of the three criteria used) we ranked tenth in the world. Such a high ranking would not be possible if we lagged behind in one of the three criteria (i.e., health). Even more impressive is the OECD Better Life Index. If you go to that site and click on "Display countries by rank," you are given the option of selecting for yourself which of the eleven factors you wish to emphasize. In the default position, the eleven all are weighted equally and the U.S., as mentioned before, ranks eighth among the thirty-eight countries ranked. But if you put maximum weight on health and give minimum weight to all other ten criteria, the U.S. jumps from eighth to sixth.

The health care system of the United States is often maligned on two fallacious grounds: the life expectancy ranking of the U.S. is forty-second out of 223 countries[105] and the infant mortality rate ranking of the U.S. is fifty-fourth out of 224 countries.[106] We shall see that the first has really nothing to do with the quality of health care available and the second is based on very misleading data from countries that count "infant lives" in very different ways.

Cardiovascular disease and cancer are by far the two leading causes of death throughout the western world. The U.S. is no exception. A nation's health system can treat those who are dealing with cardiovascular disease or cancer, but it is unrealistic to expect that same system to prevent people from the obesity that can greatly increase the risk of both cardiovascular disease and cancer. Nor can we expect the health system to prevent people from smoking or prompt them to exercise or prevent them from getting diabetes, which is a risk factor for cardiovascular disease.

When it comes to treating those dealing with cardiovascular disease and cancer, the U.S. health system is the best in the world. Sadly, however, U.S. obesity rates are the highest in the developed world. According to the OECD's own study, the U.S. has an obesity rate among those 15 years of age and over of 38.2 percent. This is very nearly double the overall average of 19.5 percent for all OECD countries.[107] That obesity is going to cause Americans to die younger, no matter the quality of the health care they receive.

Moving to the issue of smoking, Atlas writes:

> The United States had the highest level of cigarette consumption per capita compared to all other nations in the developed world over a five-decade period ending in the mid-1980s…Americans are still more significantly more likely than Western Europeans to be current or former smokers (53 percent versus 43 percent). Given the twenty-to forty-year lag time for smoking-related death and diseases, the relevance of the historical burden of cigarette consumption in the United States is noteworthy."[108]

We cannot blame the health care system for cigarette consumption.

Finally, we cannot fault the health system for the prevalence of diabetes in the United States.

Diabetes, says Atlas, "is another biological disease that is a very significant risk factor for cardiovascular diseases and a significant comorbidity for worse health outcomes generally...

> Americans harbor a greater burden from diabetes than almost all other developed countries, not just from its deleterious impact on life expectancy, but also in its tendency for worse outcomes from its many associated diseases and numerous complications...

> The higher incidence of diabetes in the United States than in other OECD nations, affects the statistics used to calculate life expectancy and lowers the U.S. rank.[109]

A health system cannot be graded on its ability to control the lifestyle choices of the citizenry, nor on any propensity toward illness that may be characteristic of a certain population. But it can be graded on how well it treats those who are afflicted with a given disease, and here the U.S. is the world leader.

Atlas provides a wealth of data showing that survival rates for almost all types of cancer are better in the U.S. than in Western Europe or Canada.[110] He also shows that the U.S. is the clear world leader in treating cardiovascular disease.[111] It is remarkable that this can be the case despite the disadvantages facing U.S. doctors in terms of working with patients more prone to be obese, be former smokers, and be afflicted with diabetes, all of which work against recovery from cancer and cardiovascular disease. There is a reason that Italian Prime Minister Silvio Berlusconi chose to have his cardiac pacemaker surgery at the Cleveland Clinic. And there is a reason that the Canadian Prime Minister of Newfoundland and Labrador, Danny Williams, traveled to the U.S. for a heart valve procedure. Williams explained, "'This was my heart, my choice and my health,' and 'I did not sign away my right to get the best possible health care for myself when I entered politics.'"[112]

Those reasons have to do with the tremendous amount of research done in the U.S. Atlas writes, "By virtually any measure, it is an inescapable conclusion that the vast majority of health care innovation comes out of the U.S. health care system, innovation from which the entire world benefits...[113]

> One striking illustration is that the top five U.S. hospitals alone conduct more clinical trials than all the hospitals in any other single developed country in the world.

> It has been estimated that 80 percent of all the innovations in health care in the world comes out of the U.S. health-care system.

> In terms of patent production and researchers in biomedical technology, the United States dominates the rest of the world.

> Since the mid-1970s, the Nobel Prize in Medicine or Physiology has gone to American scientists more often than recipients from all other countries combined.

> Ask the world's doctors where they learned the newest advances in diagnostics and therapy—the answer is nearly always the United States.[114]

A Canadian doctor, David Gratzer, associated with the conservative Manhattan Institute, echoes Atlas's observations. Gratzer points out that the United States "is the country of medical inno-vation...[We're] surrounded by medical miracles. Death by car-diovascular disease has dropped by two-thirds in the last fifty years. You've got to pay a price for that kind of advancement."[115] The rest of the world benefits by the money the U.S. pours into its health system.

I will not go into detail here, but Dr. Atlas (along with many others) has provided a wealth of data about wait times for both testing and medical procedures.

> Americans spend much less time waiting than patients in countries with nationalized, government-controlled health systems, and Americans have far greater access to mod-ern medical diagnostic tests and treatments....Data from Sweden, Canada, and the United Kingdom...reveal to even the casual observer that unconscionable waits occur for almost all important aspects of modern medical care: to see a specialist, to have a life-changing surgery like hip replacement or cataract removal, or to get radiation treat-ment for cancer.[116]

In the beginning of this chapter, I noted that the health care system in the U.S. is often maligned on two fallacious grounds: the issue of life expectancy, which we've discussed, and the infant mortality rate. The latter is fallacious because we are not comparing apples to apples when we compare our infant mortality rates with those of other countries. Different countries count "live births" in different ways, and the U.S. tends to count more births as "live births" than do other countries. For example, if the U.S. counts as a live birth a baby who lives for only a few hours after birth and another country does not, that will obviously impact infant mor-tality rates and render any direct comparison meaningless.

Still another factor that makes it impossible to compare apples to apples is the effort the U.S. makes to save preemies as early as twenty-two to twenty-three weeks' gestation. We are often told that there are twenty-five developed countries with lower infant mortality rates than the U.S., and that is true. But what often isn't said is that U.S. medical technology is more advanced than most countries when it comes to trying to save preemies. We try to save a lot of babies born at twenty-two or twenty-three weeks, whom many other countries aren't even trying to save. Of course, tragically, many of these preemies die. When you take out babies born before twenty-four weeks, only nine (not twenty-five) countries have a lower infant mortality rate than the U.S., according to the CDC, as reported on CBS News by Tara Haelle on September 24, 2014. The lead author of the CDC study, Marian MacDorman, suggests also that the tragic death of full-term babies is not likely the result of our health care system:

> The infant mortality rate specifically among early preemies (twenty-four to thirty-one weeks) was mostly similar in the United States and Europe, but the U.S. rate for babies born between thirty-two and thirty-six weeks was poorer. For babies born at thirty-seven weeks or later, the United States ranked last.

> 'These are full-term babies who presumably are pretty healthy,' MacDorman said. 'This report doesn't directly describe what's going on there, but I think it's more about social factors, such as SIDS [sudden infant death syndrome] and injuries. I don't think it's so much about health care but about the environment and raising a child.'[117]

Dr. Scott Atlas also weighs in on the subject (emphases his):

Virtually every national and international agency involved in statistical assessments of health status, health care, and economic development uses the infant-mortality rate—the number of infants per 1,000 live births who die before reaching the age of one—as a fundamental indicator. America's high infant-mortality rate has been repeatedly put forth as evidence 'proving' the substandard performance of the U.S. health-care system...

Yet it's not that simple. Infant and neonatal mortality rates are complex, multifactorial end-points that oversimplify heterogeneous inputs, many of which have no relation to health care at all. Moreover, these statistics gleaned from the widely varied countries of the world are plagued by inconsistencies, problematic definitions, and gross inaccuracies, all of which disadvantage the ranking of the U.S., where accuracy is paramount. Even though Oestergaard's WHO report lists several 'challenges and limitations' in comparing neonatal mortality rates, sensationalized headlines continue to rage about the supposedly poor showing of the United States. The following are a few of the difficulties:

Underreporting and unreliability of infant-mortality data from other countries undermine any comparisons with the United States. In a 2008 study, Joy Lawn estimated that a full three-fourths of the world's neonatal deaths are counted only through highly unreliable five-yearly retrospective household surveys, instead of being reported at the time by hospitals and health-care professionals, as in the United States. Moreover, the most premature babies—those with the highest likelihood of dying—are the least likely to be recorded in infant and neonatal mortality statistics in other countries. Compounding that difficulty, in other countries the underreporting is greatest for deaths that occur very soon after birth. Since the earliest deaths make up 75 percent of all neonatal deaths, under-reporting by other countries—often misclassifying what were really live births as fetal demise (stillbirths)—would falsely exclude most neonatal deaths. Any assumption that the practice of underreporting is confined to less-developed nations is incorrect. In fact, a number of published peer-reviewed studies show that underreporting of early neona-tal deaths has varied between 10 percent and 30 percent in highly developed Western European and Asian countries.

Gross differences in the fundamental definition of 'live birth' invalidate comparisons of early neonatal death rates. The United States strictly adheres to the WHO defi-nition of live birth (any infant 'irrespective of the duration of the pregnancy, which…breathes or shows any other evi-dence of life…whether or not the umbilical cord has been cut or the placenta is attached') and uses a strictly imple-mented linked birth and infant-death data set. On the contrary, many other nations, including highly developed countries in Western Europe, use far less strict definitions, all of which underreport the live births of more fragile infants who soon die. As a consequence, they falsely report more favorable neonatal- and infant-mortality rates.

A 2006 report from WHO stated that 'among developed countries, mortality rates may reflect differences in the definitions used for reporting births, such as cut-offs for registering live births and birth weight.' The *Bulletin* of WHO noted that 'it has also been common practice in several countries (e.g., Belgium, France, Spain) to register as live births only those infants who survived for a speci-fied period beyond birth'; those who did not survive were 'completely ignored for registration purposes.' Since the U.S. counts as live births all babies who show 'any evidence of life,' even the most premature and the smallest—the very babies who account for the majority of neonatal deaths—it necessarily has a higher neonatal-mortality rate than coun-tries that do not....

Jan Richardus showed that the perinatal mortality rate 'can vary by 50% depending on which definition is used,' and Wilco Graafmans reported that terminology differences alone among Belgium, Denmark, Finland, France, Germany, Greece, the Netherlands, Norway, Portugal, Spain, Sweden, and the U.K.—highly developed countries with substantially different infant-mortality rates—caused rates to vary by 14 to 40 percent, and generated a false reduction in reported infant-mortality rates of up to 17 percent. These differences, coupled with the fact that the U.S. medical system is far more aggressive about resuscitating very premature infants, mean that very premature infants are even more likely to be catego-rized as live births in the U.S., even though they have only a small chance of surviving. Considering that, even in the U.S., roughly half of all infant mortality occurs in the first twenty-four hours, the single factor of omitting very early deaths in many European nations generates their falsely superior neo-natal-mortality rates....

Throughout the developed world, and regardless of the health-care system, infant-mortality rates are far worse among minority populations, and the U.S. has much

more diversity of race and ethnicity than any other developed nation. Whether in wholly government-run health-care systems—like Canada's, or the U.K.'s NHS—or in the mixed U.S. system, racial and ethnic minorities have higher infant-mortality rates, roughly double those of the majority. While these disparities are among the most perplexing problems in society, they are extremely complex, identifiable even when other risk factors (including maternal age, marital status, and education) are taken into account, and often entirely separate from health-care quality. Population heterogeneity specifically distorts mortality rates in the U.S., because the racial-ethnic heterogeneity of the U.S. is far higher, four to eight times that found in Western European nations like Sweden, Norway, France, and the UK.

In summary, the analysis and subsequent comparison of neonatal- and infant-mortality rates have been filled with inconsistencies and pitfalls, problematic definitions, and inaccuracies. Even the use of the most fundamental term, 'live births,' greatly distorts infant-mortality rates, because often the infants who die the soonest after birth are not counted as live births outside the United States. In the end, these comparisons reflect deviations in fundamental terminology, reporting accuracy, data sources, populations, and cultural-medical practices—all of which specifically disadvantage the U.S. in international rankings. And unbeknownst to organizations bent on painting a picture of inferior health care in the U.S., the peer-reviewed literature and even the WHO's own statements agree.[118]

Few would argue against the idea that the U.S. health care system is in need of improvement. But whether that improvement should come in the form of more government intervention or less is at the heart of the debate. I lean toward the latter, being convinced that markets generally work better when they are relatively free of government intervention. I say relatively free because I do believe that government plays a role in helping those who fall through the cracks and in helping to correct market distortions. Liberals are more prone than conservatives to see these latter two needs.

Jonathan Haidt suggests the following analogy to explain what ails our health care system:

> The next time you go to the supermarket, look closely at a can of peas. Think about all the work that went into it—the farmers, truckers, and supermarket employees, the miners and metalworkers who made the can—and think how miraculous it is that you can buy this can for under a dollar. At every step of the way, competition among suppliers rewarded those whose innovations shaved a penny off the cost of getting that can to you. If God is commonly thought to have created the world and then arranged it for our benefit, then the free market (and its invisible hand) is a pretty good candidate for being a god...
>
> Now let's do the devils work and spread chaos throughout the marketplace. Suppose one day all prices are removed from all products in the supermarket. All labels too, beyond a simple description of the contents, so you can't compare products from different companies. You just take whatever you want, as much as you want, and you bring it up to the register. The checkout clerk scans in your food insurance card and helps you fill out your itemized claim. You pay a flat fee of $10 and go home with your groceries. A month later you get a bill informing you that your food insurance

company will pay the supermarket for most of the remaining cost, but you'll have to send in a check for an additional $15. It might sound like a bargain to get a cartload of food for $25, but you're really paying your grocery bill every month when you fork over $2,000 for your food insurance premium.

Under such a system, there is little incentive for anyone to find innovative ways to reduce the cost of food or increase its quality. The supermarket gets paid by the insurers, and the insurers get their premiums from you. The cost of food insurance begins to rise as supermarkets stock only the foods that net them the highest insurance payments, not the foods that deliver value to you.

As the cost of food insurance rises, many people can no longer afford it. Liberals...push for a new government program to buy food insurance for the poor and the elderly. But once the government becomes the major purchaser of food, then success in the supermarket and food insurance industries depends primarily on maximizing yield from government payouts. Before you know it, that can of peas costs the government $30, and all of us are paying 25 percent of our paychecks in taxes just to cover the cost of buying groceries for each other at hugely inflated costs....

As long as consumers are spared from taking price into account—that is, as long as someone else is always paying for your choices—things will get worse. We can't fix the problem by convening panels of experts to set the maximum allowable price for a can of peas. Only a working market can bring supply, demand, and ingenuity together to provide health care at the lowest possible price. For example, there is an open market for LASIK surgery...Doctors compete with one another to attract customers, and because the procedure is rarely covered by insurance, patients take price into account. Competition and innovation have driven down the price of the surgery by nearly 80 percent since it was first introduced. (Other developed nations have had more success controlling costs, but they too face rapidly rising costs that may become fiscally ruinous. Like America, they often lack the political will to raise taxes or cut services.)[119]

It is worth noting that the other developed nations mentioned by Haidt are able to control costs in part by rationing care. It is also worth noting that behind the façade of some of these socialized health care countries are private insurers catering to the well-to-do. The U.S. has much company among developed countries in needing to find a way to better serve the medical needs of the poor. I believe we have seen enough evidence in this chapter demonstrating that we are not alone among developed nations in finding that one's health care often reflects one's socioeconomic status to make the same argument that I made in the chapter on education. Try doubling, tripling, quadrupling, or quintupling the number of racial and ethnic minorities European countries have, and then see what happens to quality of health care.

Despite all the problems that plague health care here, there is much that is good about the health care system in the United States. Its ability to provide top-flight care to its own citizens as well as its role in contributing medical innovations to countries outside our borders are noteworthy moral goods. And the fact that most agree that the U.S. health care system is in need of improvement, most importantly in improving health care for the poor (a need it shares with the rest of the developed world), does not negate those moral goods.

15

On Being a Woman in the U.S.

This chapter differs from the above in that here I point out a number of concerns that we would not want to celebrate as a country. The purpose in doing so, however, is to refute the idea that women are greatly disadvantaged in our society and to suggest that male-domination is simply not the given it is often assumed to be (and once was).

Imagine a being from another galaxy being told that they were to be transported to the U.S. to live their life. They were given a choice of whether they would be male or female. Many might think this is a no-brainer. The obvious choice would be male—but I'm not sure it is quite that obvious. I'm not saying the being would choose to be female, but I think the decision is not as easy as some might think.

This being would be given a tremendous amount of data to process before making its decision (much of which might cause it to choose to be a male). Among the things it would learn that might cause it to choose to be a female are the following:

1. Women live a bit more than five years longer than men. Warren Farrell was once a member of the board of directors of the National Organization for Women and named by the *Financial Times* as one of the world's top one hundred thought leaders. He later came to believe that the feminist movement had pushed their agenda so far as to hurt men. He then became an advocate for men's rights. In a 2014 interview in *Psychology Today* he said, "We don't need a women's movement blaming men, nor a men's movement blaming women. We need a gender liberation movement. We need both sexes walking a mile in each other's moccasins." In the same interview, in response to the question, "Is the fact that men die 5.2 years younger than women another example of male disposability?" he responded, "It is the *combination* of facts like men dying 5.2 years younger than women—or men dying sooner from all ten of the ten leading causes of death—plus the fact that we have seven federal offices of women's health and none of men's health that together reflect the psychology of indifference toward male disposability. Similarly, men over the age of eighty-five commit suicide 1,350 percent as frequently as women over eighty-five. Virtually no one knows this. If women over eighty-five committed suicide 1,350 percent as often as men, it would be used as the quintessential example of our undervaluing of women..."[120]

Overall males commit suicide 257 percent more frequently than women (i.e., 3.57 times as often). And white males, while making up about 30 percent of the population, account for about 70 percent of suicides.[121] Why isn't this a huge social justice issue among progressives? It's because they are white males. Sadly, it's really that simple.

Dr. Marty Nemko teaches at the University of California at San Francisco Medical School. Formerly he taught at the University of California at Berkeley (the school from which he received his PhD) in the graduate school of education. He notes in an article on his website that "A search of more than 3,000 medical journals listed in Index Medicus found that 23 articles were written on women's health for each *one* written on men's."[122]

2. We often hear about the glass ceiling (and it might cause our being from beyond to choose to be male), but we seldom hear about what I call the "glass floor." That is the fact that twenty-four of the twenty-five most dangerous jobs are overwhelmingly manned (pun intended) by males, and that, according to the U.S. Department of Labor, 92.5 percent of workplace deaths occur to men.[123] If the situation were reversed, I have no doubt there would be a huge outcry (and rightfully so). But instead we hear almost nothing.

3. A July 1, 2016, *TIME* magazine article reported on a Harris Poll survey on happiness in which U.S. women scored 14 percent higher than U.S. men.[124]

4. We often hear the mantra about women earning 77 cents on the dollar compared to a man. President Obama dragged this out more than once. This is economic misinformation that has been debunked by a number of economists.

The Cambridge- and Oxford-educated Brett Arends has been writing for years for a number of U.S. business outlets. In 2016, he wrote the following in an opinion piece for *MarketWatch*:

> Can everyone please stop talking complete nonsense about the 'gender pay gap'?
>
> The recent 'Equal Pay Day' has produced, once again, the tedious and predictable flood of half-truths and untruths about the relative pay of men and women. But repeating something over and over doesn't make it correct. A million angry tweets do not rebut a single fact. And while it's terrific that we are on patrol against unfair discrimination,

it's terrible that we are nationally so indulgent about lazy thinking.

No, women don't get paid 79 cents on the dollar for doing the same work as men. Nothing like it. Nothing close. Sorry, folks. But that's not what the data say.

Most of that gap is explained by personal choices being made by millions of individual women and men—about whether to major in literature or economics in college, about whether to pursue a career at a nonprofit or a bank, and about whether you'd rather find yourself at 7 p.m. on a Wednesday night in February sitting at home reading a bedtime story to your children or sitting in a windowless conference room in Cleveland arguing with an obnoxious client about depreciation schedules.

Most of the choices being made are being made freely. Indeed, the gaps get bigger as you move up the socioeconomic scale, which is precisely where individuals have more power to choose.

When we focus on this 79-cents figure, we are actually being the opposite of feminist. We are embracing a traditionally 'male' perspective, where money trumps everything else. Who is to say someone has been 'disadvantaged' because they chose quality of life over more money? On the contrary, pretty much all psychological research and historical wisdom point the other way. So why are we not instead talking about a male 'gender gap' in quality of life?[125]

The question of choice is expanded on by the polymath Thomas Sowell in his book, *Economic Facts and Fallacies*.

Women have tended to make career choices influenced by the likelihood that they would at some point or other become mothers. Since motherhood has usually entailed a period of withdrawal from full-time work outside the home, the cost of such withdrawal becomes a factor in occupational choices.

Where an occupation is unionized and withdrawal from the workforce means a loss of seniority, reducing the prospects of being promoted or of being retained during lay-offs, such an occupation in effect imposes costs on women that are likely to be greater than the costs imposed on men...even some non-unionized companies may have seniority systems which have the same economic effect, reducing women's earnings prospects more than those of men. Seniority is often also a factor in civil service jobs, likewise reducing women's earnings prospects more than those of men.

Interruptions in labor force participation have other costs which fall disproportionately on women. The occupational skills required change over time and at varying rates for different occupations...

From the standpoint of a young woman looking ahead when making career choices, the relative rates of obsolescence of given knowledge and skills in a given field becomes a serious consideration in choosing a field in which to specialize. It has been estimated that a physicist loses half the value of his or her knowledge in four years, while a professor of English would take more than a quarter of a century to lose half the value of the knowledge with which he or she began that career.

Given the asymmetrical effects of career obsolescence on women and men, it is hardly surprising that women tend to work in fields with lower rates of obsolescence—as teachers and librarians, for example, rather than as computer engineers or tax accountants. Even as the proportion of women receiving PhDs rose dramatically from the 1970s on, male-female differences in fields of specialization remained large.

While many jobs have regular nine-to-five hours, many others require putting in whatever hours happen to be required, whenever and wherever they happen to be required. When a multi-million dollar lawsuit is in progress or a death penalty case is being appealed, the attorneys involved cannot simply quit work at five o'clock and go home. If the case requires working nights and weekends, then the attorneys have to work nights and weekends...

In principle it does not matter whether the attorney is male or female but, in practice, with women more often than men carrying the burden of domestic responsibilities for children and the care of the home, careers that involve much unpredictable night and weekend work are less attractive to women...

This may not put a whole profession off-limits but it can restrict the range of work situations within a given profession...

The most important reason why women earn less than men is not that they are paid less for doing the very same work but that they are distributed differently among jobs and have fewer hours and less continuity in the labor force. Among college-educated, never married individuals with no children who worked full-time and were from forty to sixty-four years old—that is, beyond the child-bearing years—men averaged $40,000 a year in income, while women averaged $47,000....

Much also depends on whether the goal should be equal opportunities or equal incomes. As Professor Claudia Goldin, an economist at Harvard, put it, 'Is equality of income what we really want? Do we want everyone to have an equal chance to work eighty hours in their prime reproductive years? Yes, but we don't expect them to take that chance equally often.'[126]

The economist Diana Furchtgott-Roth of the Manhattan Institute writes:

Progressives often claim that women earn 77 cents for every dollar that men earn. But this statistic looks only at raw averages and does not take into account factors such as education, skills, and hours worked. After controlling for other factors, the gender pay gap practically disappears. Indeed, among single, childless workers under thirty, women earn *more* than men [emphasis hers]...

Consider the following. The DOL [Department of Labor] classifies 'full-time' work as any workweek of more than thirty-five hours; but men typically work more hours than women. Among full-time workers, men work forty-three hours per week, on average, and women, forty-one hours per week. Women who work exactly forty hours per week earn 89% percent of what their respective male peers earn. (When unmarried, childless workers under thirty are compared, a 'reverse wage gap' appears, with woman earning $1.08 for every dollar earned by comparable men.)

She goes on to note that the causes of the remaining gap are numerous. Men tend to major in subjects (engineering, for example) that lead to higher paying jobs. A statistically insignificant number of petroleum-engineering majors are women and only 7 percent of electrical-engineering majors are women. Meanwhile, women account for 56 percent of drama majors, 59 percent of studio-art majors, and 88 percent of elementary-education majors. Furthermore, "women are also more likely to leave the labor force temporarily to raise children, which contributes to the work-experience gap between men and women…In a 2016 paper, Francine Blau and Lawrence Kahn of Cornell University find that 'recent research suggests a continued and important role for workforce interruptions and shorter hours in explaining gender wage gaps in high-skilled occupations.'"

Interestingly, "when part-time workers are compared in apples-to-apples fashion, the wage gap is reversed: women earn $1.03 for every dollar earned by comparable men."[127]

Are women making their choice of major because of pressure to avoid the so-called STEM majors? Not at all. In fact, schools have worked zealously to try to attract women into the STEM fields. Women are free to pursue any college major they wish. And those who take the STEM route often have an advantage over men. In a different article, Diana Furchtgott-Roth writes:

> Women who prepare for science and engineering are well rewarded in a job market that traditionally had been male-dominated. One 2010 study found that while women represented 11 percent and 12 percent of tenure-track applicants in electrical engineering and physics, they received 32

percent and 20 percent of job offers. They were more likely than male applicants to get hired when they applied. This shows that in the sciences, employers seek to remedy the traditional gender imbalance by seeking out bright women who benefit from affirmative action.[128]

Interviewed in the May–June 2016 issue of *Harvard Magazine*, Harvard economist Claudia Goldin gives one example of the way in which women make lifestyle choices in which they choose to garner things like better benefits, more flexible hours, and more time off in exchange for less pay:

> Consider a couple graduating together from a prestigious law school, and taking highly paid jobs at firms that demand long hours. The evidence suggests they're likely to begin at similar salaries. But a few years later, Goldin says, one of them—more likely the woman—may decide to leave for a smaller practice with fewer hours and more flexibility in scheduling. In that new job, research suggests, she's likely to earn less per hour than her partner.[129]

Sowell gives us an example from the medical world:

> Very substantial income differences between men and women in a particular field can co-exist with little or no income differences between women and men who are comparable within that field. For example, a study published in the *New England Journal of Medicine* found: 'In 1990, young male physicians earned 41 percent more per year than young female physicians....However, after adjusting for differences in specialty, practice setting, and other characteristics, no earnings difference was evident...'[130]

The importance of women choosing benefits over pay in explaining the "wage gap" has been documented by many. We find in a 2011 report from the Federal Reserve Bank of St. Louis, "Economists Eric Solberg and Teresa Laughlin applied an index of total compensation, which accounts for both wages and benefits, to analyze how these benefits would affect the gender gap. They found a gender gap in wages of approximately 13 percent. But when they considered total compensation, the gender gap dropped to 3.6 percent."[131]

It should be noted that the few pennies women fall short is not necessarily the result of discrimination. It may be the result of factors not yet identified. Apart from the fact that gender pay discrimination is illegal and can lead to lawsuits against those who engage in it (which is not to deny that it still can take place), logic says that if employers could get away with paying females significantly less, they would be fools to hire males.

Finally, Christina Hoff Summers notes that feminists (which she, herself, identifies as) have waved the wage gap flag for too long. "A thorough 2009 study by the US Department of Labor examined more than fifty peer-reviewed papers on the subject and concluded that the wage gap 'may be almost entirely the result of individual choices being made by both male and female workers'...There were so many differences in pay-related choices that the researchers were unable to specify even a residual effect that might be the result of discrimination."[132]

5. It would probably shock most people to learn that more than 50 percent of the victims of intimate partner physical violence are men and that more than 40 percent of the victims of *severe* physical violence by a partner are men (it certainly shocked me). The following comes from the summary of a CDC report by Bert Hoff: "According to a 2010 national survey by the Centers for Disease Control and Department of Justice, in

the last twelve months more men than women were victims of intimate partner physical violence and over 40 percent of severe physical violence was directed at men. Men were also more often the victim of psychological aggression and control over sexual or reproductive health."[133]

This problem, which draws almost no attention, is not unique to the United States. A Sept. 4, 2010, article in The Guardian states that "Data from Home Office statistical bulletins and the British Crime Survey show that men made up about 40% of domestic violence victims each year in the UK between 2004–05 and 2008–09, the last year for which figures are available."[134]

Several years ago, I suggested to my denomination, the United Church of Christ, that they report these numbers as a way of drawing attention to a largely unknown issue of justice. They would not even respond to me. It doesn't fit their template of woman = good, man = bad.

Even more shocking, perhaps, is new research which reveals that the long-held assumptions that rape is overwhelmingly a crime victimizing women and committed by men may need to be rethought. The following is the opening of an article in the *Atlantic* (November 28, 2016):

> Two years ago, Lara Stemple, Director of UCLA's Health and Human Rights Law Project, came upon a statistic that surprised her: In incidents of sexual violence reported to the National Crime Victimization Survey, 38 percent of victims were men—a figure much higher than in prior surveys. Intrigued, she began to investigate: Was sexual violence against men more common than previously thought?
>
> The inquiry was a timely one. For years, the FBI definition of rape was gendered, requiring 'carnal knowledge

of a female forcibly and against her will.' But a recent redefinition focused instead on forced penetration with no mention of gender. Meanwhile, other data-gatherers had started to track a new category of sexual violence that the Centers for Disease Control call 'being forced to penetrate.' And still others were keeping better track of sexual violence in prisons.

Taken together, the new data challenged widely held beliefs."[135]

The article quoted from a peer-reviewed study by Andrew Flores and Ilan Meyer which concluded, "'These surveys have reached many tens of thousands of people, and each has shown internally consistent results over time,' the authors note. 'We therefore believe that this article provides more definitive estimates about the prevalence of female sexual perpetration than has been provided in the literature to date. Taken as a whole, the reports we examine document surprisingly significant prevalence of female-perpetrated sexual victimization, mostly against men and occasionally against women.'"

Another study showed that when a childhood victim has experienced sexual abuse from people of both genders, they are "more reluctant to disclose the victimization perpetrated by women (Sgroi & Sargent, 1993). Indeed, the discomfort of reporting child sexual victimization by a female perpetrator can be so acute that a victim may instead inaccurately report that his or her abuser was male (Longdon, 1993)."[136]

Sadly, males who are victimized sometimes become viewed as the abuser. "Particularly as male victims move from childhood to adolescence, they are ascribed more blame for encounters with adult women." And "when female abusers are reported, they are less likely to be investigated, arrested, or punished compared to male perpetrators, who are regarded as more harmful."[137]

Clearly a number of assumptions about gender will have to be overturned before society will be able to even come close to rendering justice with regard to forced sexual acts. We are probably a long way from being able to view women as capable of the kind of aggression and sexual violence we have generally ascribed almost solely to men.

6. In the 2016–17 school year, women earned 33 percent more bachelor's degrees than men (this difference is projected to grow to 38 percent in ten years). The last time men earned more bachelor's degrees than women was the 1980–81 school year. If you go back to the 1970–71 school year, men earned 31 percent more bachelor's degrees than women, almost a mirror image of the picture today.[138] That was a problem then. The reverse should be seen as a problem now. If you expand beyond bachelor's degrees to include everything from AA degrees to PhDs, women now earn more degrees at each level than do men. In fact, that has been the case for several years:

> According to data from the Department of Education on college degrees by gender, the U.S. college degree gap favoring women started back in 1978, when for the first time ever, more women than men earned associate's degrees. Five years later in 1982, women earned more bachelor's degrees than men for the first time, and women have increased their share of bachelor's degrees in every year since then. In another five years by 1987, women earned the majority of master's degrees for the first time. Finally, within another decade, more women than men earned doctor's degrees by 2006, and female domination of college degrees at every level was complete.[139]

Their math is a little off: 1987–2006 is not "another decade," but the point is made.

Are grade schools, middle schools, and high schools doing anything near to what they would be doing if the discrepancy was the other way around? More to the point, are they doing what *was* done when the discrepancy *was* the other way around?

7. Sonja Starr, a professor of law at the University of Michigan Law School, has studied gender disparity in the federal court system and found that men receive sentences that are 63 percent higher, on average, than their female counterparts. She also found that females arrested for a crime are significantly more likely to avoid charges and convictions entirely, and twice as likely to avoid incarceration if convicted.[140]

8. Dr. Nemko wrote an article titled "The Problem With Boys: An ignored crisis" which appeared in the September 20, 2014, issue of *Psychology Today*. He begins as follows:

> What changes would you recommend if you were told that African-American children were:
>
> - Four to eight times as likely to be drugged with Ritalin and other stimulants which pediatrician Leonard Sax calls 'academic steroids.'
> - Reading much more poorly than are other students.
> - Three times as likely to commit suicide.
> - 2½ times as likely to drop out of high school.
> - Severely underrepresented in college and even more so among college graduates, thereby locking them out of today's, let alone tomorrow's professional-level jobs.
>
> You'd likely invoke such words as 'institutional racism' to justify major efforts to improve African-American numbers.

All of the above statements are true except for one thing: those statistics aren't about African-American children. They're about children of all races, indeed half of all children, half of our next generation: boys.[141]

Nearly three years later, in June 2017, another contributor to *Psychology Today*, Dr. Rob Whitley, suggested that we haven't learned much:

> Men's Health Month [Did you even know there was a Men's Health Month? I didn't.] generally passes not with a bang but a whimper. The same can be said for attention given to inequalities experienced by boys and young men. These inequalities are rarely on the public radar, despite a massive cost to the affected boys and society as a whole.
>
> Seeing reality is the first step towards changing it. Raising awareness is a start, but concrete measures are necessary to increase the well-being, mental health and social inclusion of boys and young men.
>
> We may very well be in the midst of a boy's crisis. If so, inaction is not an option.[142]

Christina Hoff Sommers has devoted a book to the problem of boys falling farther and farther behind girls in the classroom. In *The War Against Boys*, we learn that the school environment has becoming increasingly anti-male. This can be seen from the classroom to the playground.

In the classroom, boys are being given fewer and fewer stories to read featuring adventurous male heroes. It can be little wonder that girls are extending their already considerable advantage in reading skills. "Mark Bauerlein, former director of research at the National Endowment for the Arts, and Sandra Stotsky, professor of education at the University of Arkansas, summed up 'Why Johnny Won't Read' in a 2005 *Washington Post* op-ed: 'Unfortunately, the textbooks and literature assigned in the elementary grades do not reflect the dispositions of male students. Few strong and active male role models can be found as lead characters...Publishers seem to be more interested in avoiding 'masculine' perspectives or 'stereotypes' than in getting boys to like what they are assigned to read.'"[143]

> "What," asks Sommers, "finally, explains boys' plight in education? Why should they be so far behind girls in honors courses and college attendance? Boys score slightly better than girls on national math and science tests—yet their grades in these subjects are lower. They perform worse than girls on literacy tests—but their classroom grades are even lower than these test scores predict. How does that happen?"

The answer Sommers finds in research done by others is that:

> Teachers *as early as kindergarten* factor good behavior into grades—and girls, as a rule, comport themselves far better and are more amenable to classroom routines than boys... Non-cognitive skills include self-control, attentiveness, organization, and the ability to sit still for long periods of time. As most parents know, girls tend to develop these skills earlier and more naturally than boys do...

> Some will say: too bad for the boys. If young boys are inattentive, obstreperous, and upsetting to their teachers, that's their problem. As one critic told me, the classroom is no

more rigged against boys than workplaces are rigged against lazy and unfocused workers.

But unfocused workers are adults. We are talking here about children as young as five or six. If little boys are restless and unfocused, why not look for ways to help them improve? When we realized that girls, as a group, were languishing behind boys in math and science, we mounted a concerted national effort to give female students more support and encouragement, and effort that has met with significant success. Surely we should try to provide similar help to boys. Much is at stake.

Grades, more than ever before, are crucially important to a child's future…

Boys, on average, lack the social maturity of girls—and for that, many are paying a high price that continues after they have become more purposive young adults. What is the answer? More boy-friendly curricula? More male teachers? More single-sex classrooms? Special preschool classes to improve boys' social skills? Extra recess where boys are allowed to engage in their characteristic rough-and-tumble play?…As we will see in chapters to come, these are all promising solutions—and all are strenuously opposed by the women's lobby.

Teachers know that their male students are struggling, and most would welcome new ideas on how to help them. But they get little help or support from official circles. The 2012 *Gender Equity in Education* report is striking proof that boys are nowhere on the agenda.

The sad truth is that the educational deficits of boys may be one of the least studied phenomena in American education...[144]

Let us look briefly at another subject Sommers brings up: recess. Recess may someday go the way of oil lamps. Sommers reports a 25 percent decrease in play and a 50 percent decrease in unstructured outdoor activities.[145] The city of Atlanta did away with recess in all its public elementary schools in 1998. Schools are built without playgrounds. Some other cities have followed suit. Whether that will turn out to be a trend that catches on widely remains to be seen. What has caught on in many schools is a tendency to make recess less boy-friendly. Sommers writes:

Many games much loved by boys have vanished from school playgrounds. At some elementary schools, tug of war is being replaced with 'tug-of-peace'....

The new therapeutic sensibility rejects almost all forms of competition in favor of a gentle and nurturing climate of cooperation. It is also a surefire way to bore and alienate boys.

From the earliest age, boys show a distinct preference for active outdoor play, with a strong predilection for games with body contact, conflict, and clearly defined winners and losers.

Anthony Pellegrini, a professor of early childhood education at the University of Minnesota, defines rough-and-tumble play (R&T) as a behavior that includes 'laughing, running, smiling, jumping, open-hand beating, wrestling, play fighting, chasing and fleeing.' This type of play is often mistakenly regarded as aggression, but according to

Pellegrini, R&T is the very opposite. In cases of school-yard aggression, the participants are unhappy, they part as enemies, and there are often tears and injuries. Rough-and-tumble play brings boys together, makes them happy, and is a critical part of their socialization.

'Children who engaged in R&T, typically boys, also tended to be liked and to be good social problem solvers,' says Pellegrini. Aggressive children, on the other hand, tend not to be liked by their peers and are not good at solving problems. He urges parents and teachers to be aware of the differences between R&T and aggression. The former is educationally and developmentally important and should be permitted and encouraged; the latter is destructive and should not be allowed.[146]

The very thought that there might be innate differences between the sexes will draw ire from many in academia. When Harvard president Lawrence Summers merely speculated about the idea that innate differences between the sexes might have something to do with why we see more men than women in the highest positions of science, the over-the-top response included a conference at Harvard where, instead of a dialogue taking place, the six panelists simply pronounced that the only possible explanation for the phenomenon about which Summers was speculating was sexism. I have to wonder if they were as irate when an article titled "Are Women More Ethical Than Men?" appeared in the June 11, 2014, issue of *Psychology Today*. I happen to believe that the question raised by the article is a legitimate one, worthy of study. But then, I also believe that the question raised by Summers was legitimate.

One panelist, Harvard psychologist Elizabeth Spelke, flatly declared that the case against significant inborn cognitive differences 'is as conclusive as any finding I know of in science.'

For any scholar," writes Sommers, "especially a Harvard University social scientist, to sweep aside all evidence for innate differences defies belief. In 2010, David Geary, a University of Missouri psychologist, published, *Male, Female: The Evolution of Human Sex Differences*. This thorough, fair-minded, and comprehensive survey of the literature includes more than fifty pages of footnotes citing studies by neuroscientists, endocrinologists, geneticists, anthropologists, and psychologists showing a strong biological basis for many gender differences. While these particular studies may not be the final word, they cannot be dismissed or ignored.

Nor can human reality be tossed aside. In all known societies, women have better verbal skills, and men excel at spatial reasoning. Women tend to be the nurturers and men the warriors. Harvard psychologist Steven Pinker points to the absurdity of ascribing these universal differences to socialization: 'It would be an amazing coincidence that in every society the coin flip that assigns each sex to one set of roles would land the same way.'[147]

I suspect you can keep giving dolls to baby boys until you're blue in the face (or pink, if you prefer), but they will still, more often than not, reach for the toy cars. And vice versa with girls.

I don't pretend to know what gender our hypothetical being would end up choosing. But I would suggest that it's not a shut-and-closed case that the being would choose to be male. A wise individual might well choose to be female. Neither decision would surprise me. This situation is a far cry from what it would have been sixty years ago. Then our hypothetical being would have chosen in all likelihood to be a man. Much of what I have written in this chapter might not seem like something to celebrate. But I have written it to make the point that there have been tremendous strides made by women in the last half century. Sometimes a moral good has to be accomplished by starting to move the pendulum. That inevitably raises the risk of the pendulum swinging too far, at least on some issues. Sommers views the historical feminist movement as a great thing. I agree with her. I also agree with her that the time is long overdue to show some concern for the situation of men and boys in our society. That said, the remarkable progress made by women in the last half century is a moral good.

CHAPTER 16

The Sandbox Metaphor

Imagine that you are by far the biggest person in a sandbox filled with much smaller people. You will inevitably step on some toes. If you are a good person, you will try to break up fights, but in doing so you will always run the risk of mistakenly siding with the party in the wrong rather than with the wronged party. You will take some blows yourself in the process. You will begin to notice which of the people in the sandbox with you are forces for good, which are largely indifferent to what goes on about them, and which are forces for evil. You will want to limit the evil done by those inclined in that direction and work toward persuading the indifferent to see that the sandbox can be a better place if all in the sandbox respect the principles of sandbox etiquette. To do so, you will form coalitions to work toward making the sandbox a place of greater good. With skill and some luck, you will succeed.

The United States has been that biggest person in the sandbox since 1945 and—not without mistakes and setbacks—it has succeeded spectacularly in helping the world to achieve peace and prosperity to an unprecedented degree.

Arguably, the three greatest threats to the existence of a free world over the course of the last century were Nazism, Japanese imperialism, and Communism (be it of the Soviet or Chinese variety). That these threats are largely ghosts of the past and that the free world has grown in expanse, is due, in varying degrees, to the efforts of the United States. The defeat of the Nazis, of course, was the work of many countries. Ironically, no country sacrificed more lives in that effort than the Soviet Union, only for it to become an even greater threat to the free world. Likewise, the defeat of Japanese imperialism was the work of many countries, although the U.S. played by far the greatest role. However, neither the Nazis nor Imperial Japan posed the threat to the free world that the Soviet Union posed. And only the United States was in a position to counter them. Because the U.S. bore the greatest financial burden in countering Soviet totalitarianism, other developed nations have been free to put their resources elsewhere.

Freedom House, a U.S.-based 501 U.S. Government-funded non-governmental organization, began monitoring freedom around the world in 1972. In that year they determined that 29 percent of the nations of the world were free, 25 percent were partly free, and 46 percent were not free. Fast forward to 2016 and we find 45 percent of the nations of the world recognized as free, 30 percent partly free, and 25 percent not free.[148] Thanks to the umbrella of protection provided by the U.S., and the U.S. winning the Cold War, the number of nations that can be regarded as free has grown significantly over the last forty-four years (though the last ten years have seen a very slight decline). And that same umbrella of protection has kept free those that were already free prior to 1972. Of course, if we go back to 1945, before Freedom House was monitoring freedom, the number of free nations would have been miniscule. Even the 29 percent of 1972 that now seems puny would have seemed miraculous in 1945. On a related note, 90 percent of global trade travels by sea, and since World War II the U.S. has been the sole country with a navy capable of keeping the sea lanes free.

As the biggest person in the sandbox, the U.S. has made possible an unparalleled history of peace and prosperity across wide swaths of the globe over the last seventy years, greatly expanding on the early progress made possible by the Enlightenment (which itself was astonishing). This accomplishment is noted by Robert Kagan in the June 9, 2014, issue of the liberal *New Republic* (Kagan has been identified by some as a neoconservative, but calls himself a liberal interventionist):

> So Americans for more than four decades proved willing to support the expansive and active foreign policy that Roosevelt and his advisers had envisioned—indeed, probably much more than they envisioned—and the results were extraordinary. In the half-century following World War II, the United States successfully established, protected, and advanced a liberal world order, carving out a vast 'free world' within which an unprecedented era of peace and prosperity could flower in Western Europe, East Asia, and the Western Hemisphere. Although tensions between the United States and the Soviet Union sometimes rose to dangerous levels, the period was characterized above all by peace among the great powers. The United States and the Soviet Union did not come to blows, and just as importantly, the American presence in Europe and East Asia put an end to the cycles of war that had torn both regions since

the late nineteenth-century. The number of democracies in the world grew dramatically. The international trading system expanded and deepened. There was no shortage of disasters and near-disasters, as well as two costly wars in Asia—but the strategy was largely successful, so much so that the Soviet empire finally collapsed or voluntarily withdrew, peacefully, under the pressure of the West's economic and political success, and the liberal order then expanded to include the rest of Europe and most of Asia. All of this was the result of many forces—the political and economic integration of Europe, the success of Japan and Germany, and the rise of other Asian economies—but none of it would have been possible without a United States willing and able to play the abnormal and unusual role of preserver and defender of a liberal world order.[149]

The biggest man in the sandbox did not rest after the Cold War had ended. Kagan, again:

In the decade following the fall of the Berlin Wall, moreover, the United States also conducted a number of sizeable military operations—seven to be precise, roughly one every seventeen months: in Panama (1989), Iraq (1991), Somalia (1992), Haiti (1994), Bosnia (1995), Iraq again (1998), and Kosovo (1999). None were a response to perceived threats to vital national interests. All aimed at defending and extending the liberal world order—by toppling dictatorships, reversing coups, and attempting to restore democracies in Panama and Haiti; preventing mass killing or starvation in Somalia, Bosnia, and Kosovo; deterring or reversing aggression in the Persian Gulf in 1991; and attempting to prevent the proliferation of nuclear or other weapons of mass destruction in Iraq in 1998. When Bush sent thirty-thousand troops to remove the corrupt dictator Manuel Noriega, it was not, as George Will wrote approvingly at the time, in order to pursue national interests 'narrowly construed,' but to fulfill 'the rights and responsibilities that come with the possession of great power.' When Bush then carried out in Somalia what was arguably the most purely humanitarian, and therefore most purely selfless, intervention in American history, he told the public, 'I understand that the United States alone cannot right the world's wrongs.' But the 'people of Somalia need...our help' and 'some crises in the world cannot be resolved without American involvement.'

The United States, in short, was the 'indispensable nation,' as Bill Clinton would proclaim—indispensable, that is, to the preservation of a liberal world order. Such was the thinking behind most of Clinton's foreign policy initiatives...After the massacre at Srebnica in 1995, Clinton officials argued, according to David Halberstam, that 'Serb aggression' was intolerable—not because it threatened American interests directly, which obviously it did not, but because it tore at 'the very fabric of the West.'...

At the end of the day, George W. Bush's decision to remove Saddam Hussein, whether that decision was wise or foolish, was driven more by concerns for world order than by narrow self-interest. Of all the American interventions in the post-Cold War era, only the invasion of Afghanistan could be understood as directly related to America's own national security.[150]

In hindsight, I find it regrettable that George W. Bush placed so much emphasis on weapons of mass destruction as the justification for the invasion of Iraq. There were many people at that time, liberals and conservatives alike, making a humanitarian case for overthrowing Saddam Hussein. The man and his henchmen had persecuted, raped, and/or killed millions of Iraqis. The case for overthrowing him was so strong that many forget there were thirty-eight nations that supported our effort.[151]

Go back in your mind to 1945 and ask yourself, "Would I have wanted the biggest person in the sandbox to have been the Soviet Union?" There was no other choice.

The Harvard University political scientist Samuel P. Huntington (a lifelong Democrat who served in the Carter administration) talks about a wave of democratization in the Carter-Reagan years. During that decade-and-a-half, he writes:

> It would appear that U.S. support was critical to democratization in the Dominican Republic, Grenada, El Salvador, Guatemala, Honduras, Uruguay, Peru, Ecuador, Panama, and the Philippines and that it was a contributing factor to democratization in Portugal, Chile, Poland, Korea, Bolivia, and Taiwan.[152]

The overwhelming conclusion to be drawn at the end of the day is that the world, since World War II, has witnessed the greatest growth in freedom and prosperity ever seen in a seventy-year year period (more, in fact, than the history of the world up until 1800 had seen). And more than any other nation or group of nations, the United States made it possible. That may be the greatest moral good we have covered in this book.

Conclusion

I invite you to try the following thought experiment: imagine you could go back in time to 1945, remove the U.S. from the world scene, and then run history again. Would the world be a better place or a worse place? I believe it would be incalculably worse, and I believe I have presented sufficient evidence in the above chapters to make that case. There are, of course, many other countries that, were they removed, would also make the world a worse place. But there is not one country whose removal would be as catastrophic for the good of the world as would be the removal of the United States. This is not because we are "better" than other countries, but simply a function of our size and strength that allowed us to defend the free world (as argued in the previous chapter). I have no doubt that many other countries, given our position, would have done the same. Maybe some would have even made fewer mistakes. But give the United States credit. How many countries in the history of the world, given our capacity for power, have acted as magnanimously? But also give credit to those European nations whose ideas gave birth to the principles we continue to aim to live up to (and who continue to push us to be better).

We have certainly stumbled about the sandbox at times, but I am reminded of the famous quip attributed to Winston Churchill: "You can always count on Americans to do the right thing—after they've tried everything else." That is not literally true, of course. The United States hasn't always done the right thing. Churchill knew that. But he also knew that if he could pick one country to be in the trenches with him, he would want the United States by his side.

Some may wonder why I haven't mentioned Donald Trump. I left him out deliberately because I wanted to emphasize that these chapters are all about long-term trends. Could the turmoil the country has gone through during Trump's administration negatively impact some of the above? Perhaps. Maybe we'll drop a few places in the UN Happiness Report. Maybe a few less people will want to emigrate here. In any event, the U.S. has always been a very resilient nation and what goes down will likely go up again. And even if it doesn't, the U.S. is still a good nation.

I don't imagine that everyone has found all of the moral goods that I have associated with the U.S. to be compelling. My hope is that some of them have rung true and others, even if you disagree with me, have given you something to think about. I believe this is an important task, because a nation that truly believes it is worthless will not have the will to move forward in a manner that will make our world a better place. The Liberty Bell may not be physically able to ring, but it speaks a truth Traci Blackmon and those who think like her do not have the moral imagination to hear.

You are free to write a scathing rebuttal, and you may even choose to demonize the United States. But as you do so, remember that few Cubans demonized their country under Castro and got away with it. Few Chileans demonized their country under Pinochet and got away with it. Few Soviets demonized their country under Stalin and got away with it. Sadly, the same could be said for many other countries. Feel free to demonize the United States, but in doing so at least recognize the irony that the very act of being able to do so is just one more ringing of the bell of American moral goodness.

References

1. Traci Blackmon, "Commentary: A Crack in the Liberty Bell: Why Freedom Cannot Ring," *United Church of Christ News*, June 30, 2016, http://www.ucc.org/commentary_a_crack_in_the_liberty_bell_why_freedom_cannot_ring_06302016 (last accessed February 10, 2018).
2. Alec Tyson, "Most Americans think that the U.S. is great, but fewer say it is the greatest," Pew Research Center, July 2, 2014, http://www.pewresearch.org/fact-tank/2014/07/02/most-americans-think-the-u-s-is-great-but-fewer-say-its-the-greatest/ (last accessed February 7, 2018).
3. Williams, Janice, "White Men Vs. Black Men Prison Statistics 2016: Why Are More African American Males Incarcerated?," *International Business Times*, October 5, 2016, http://www.ibtimes.com/white-men-vs-black-men-prison-statistics-2016-why-are-more-african-american-males-2426793 (last accessed February 7, 2018).

4. McIntyre, Catherine, "Canada Has Black Incarceration Problem," *Torontoist*, April 21, 2016, https://torontoist.com/2016/04/african-canadian-prison-population/ (last accessed February 7, 2018).

5. Kentish, Benjamin, "Revealed: How 'racial bias' at the heart of the criminal justice system means black people in UK more likely to be in prison than those in the U.S.," *Independent*, Sept. 7, 2017, http://www.independent.co.uk/news/uk/home-news/black-people-prison-uk-more-likely-us-lammy-review-a7935061.html. (last accessed February 7, 2018).

6. Andrew Hammel, "'Other People's Indians' and German's Minority-Filled Prisons," July 26, 2015, http://andrewhammel.typepad.com/german_joys/2015/07/other-peoples-indians-and-germanys-minority-filled-prisons.html (last accessed February 9, 2018).

7. Index Mundi, "Germany Demographics Profile 2018" https://www.indexmundi.com/germany/demographics_profile.html (last accessed February 10, 2018).

8. GovUK, April 3, 2016 Press Release, "BME employment reaches record high," https://www.gov.uk/government/news/bme-employment-reaches-record-high (last accessed February 8, 2018).

9. United States Department of Labor, September, 2016 Report, "Labor force characteristics by race and ethnicity, 2015," https://www.bls.gov/opub/reports/race-and-ethnicity/2015/home.htm (last accessed February 8, 2018).

10. Jonathan Haidt, *The Righteous Mind: Why Good People are Divided by Politics and Religion* (New York: Vintage Books, 2012), pp. 358-360.

11. Walter Williams, "Black Slavery Is Alive," December 18, 2000, http://econfaculty.gmu.edu/wew/articles/00/slavery.html (last accessed February 9, 2018).

12. United States Census Bureau, 2016 figures, (last accessed February 9, 2018).

13. USA Life Expectancy, http://www.worldlifeexpectancy.com/usa/ life-expectancy-native-american (last accessed February 9, 2018).

14. United States Census Bureau, 2016 figures, https://www.census. gov/quickfacts/fact/table/US/PST045217#viewtop (last accessed February 9, 2018).

15. USA Life Expectancy, http://www.worldlifeexpectancy.com/usa/ life-expectancy-asian-american (last accessed February 9, 2018).

16. United States Census Bureau, 2016 figures, https://www.census. gov/quickfacts/fact/table/US/PST045217#viewtop (last accessed February 9, 2018).

17. USA Life Expectancy, http://www.worldlifeexpectancy.com/usa/ life-expectancy-african-american (last accessed February 9, 2018).

18. United States Census Bureau, 2016 figures, https://www.census. gov/quickfacts/fact/table/US/PST045217#viewtop (last accessed February 9, 2018).

19. USA Life Expectancy, http://www.worldlifeexpectancy.com/usa/ life-expectancy-hispanic (last accessed February 9, 2018).

20. USA Life Expectancy, http://www.worldlifeexpectancy.com/usa/ life-expectancy-native-american (last accessed February 9, 2018).

21. Joel Achenbach, "Life expectancy improves for blacks, and the racial gap is closing," *The Washington Post*, May 2, 2017, https:// www.washingtonpost.com/news/to-your-health/wp/2017/05/02/ cdc-life-expectancy-up-for-blacks-and-the-racial-gap-is- closing/?utm_term=.6ee8850f028b (last accessed February 11, 2018).

22. Mark Trahant, "Measuring the Progress in Native Health – Life Expectancy for Native Americans," *HUFFPOST*, July 4, 2010 updated December 6, 2017, https://www.huffingtonpost. com/mark-trahant/measuring-the-progress-in_b_562274.html (last accessed February 11, 2018).

23. Neil Esipuva, Julie Ray and Anita Pugliese, "Number of Potential Migrants Worldwide Tops 700 Million," *Gallup News*, June 8, 2017, http://news.gallup.com/poll/211883/number-potential-migrants-worldwide-tops-700-million.aspx (last accessed February 11, 2018).

24. Mark Lewis, "More Americans migrated to Norway than the other way around in 2016," *Chicago Tribune*, January 13, 2018, https://www.google.com/search?q=more+americans+migrated+to+norway+than+the+other+way+around&rlz=1C1NHXL_enUS721US721&oq=more&aqs=chrome.1.69i57j35i39j69i65j69i61l2j35i39.2565j1j4&sourceid=chrome&ie=UTF-8 (last accessed March 20, 2018).

25. Asian Pacific Foundation of Canada, "Canadians Abroad," 2011, http://www.asiapacific.ca/sites/default/files/canadians_abroad_final.pdf (last accessed March 20, 2018).

26. Tom Turula, "More than 7% of Swedes live abroad and USA is their favorite country," *Business Insider*, January 5, 2007, http://nordic.businessinsider.com/more-than-7-of-swedish-natives-live-abroad--and-usa-is-their-favorite-country-2017-1 (last accessed March 20, 2018).

27. The Federal Council, "Swiss nationals living abroad," https://www.eda.admin.ch/countries/china/en/home/living-in/swiss-nationals-living-abroad.html (last accessed March 20, 2018).

28. Asia Matters for America, "Australians in America and Americans in Australia," http://www.asiamattersforamerica.org/australia/data/population (last accessed March 20, 2018).

29. Nathan Siegel, "Dozens Of Countries Take In More Immigrants Per Capita Than The U.S.," *npr*, October 29, 2014, https://www.npr.org/2014/10/29/359963625/dozens-of-countries-take-in-more-immigrants-per-capita-than-the-u-s (last accessed February 11, 2018).

30. Ibid, (last accessed March 20, 2018).

31. Australian Bureau of Statistics, "Migration, Australia, 2015-16," March 30. 2017, http://www.abs.gov.au/ausstats/abs@.nsf/mf/3412.0 (last accessed February 11, 2018).

32. Statistics New Zealand, "2013 QuickStats About culture and Identity," p.20, file:///C:/Users/Owner/Downloads/quickstats-culture-identity.pdf (last accessed February 11, 2018).

33. Statistics Canada, "Immigration and Ethnocultural Diversity Highlight Tables," http://www12.statcan.gc.ca/census-recensement/2016/dp-pd/hlt-fst/imm/Table.cfm?Lang=E&T=21&Geo=01&SO=4D (last accessed February 13, 2018).

34. US Census Bureau American FactFinder, "PLACE OF BIRTH FOR THE FOREIGN-BORN POPULATION IN THE UNITED STATES," https://factfinder.census.gov/faces/tableservices/jsf/pages/productview.xhtml?pid=ACS_16_1YR_B05006&prodType=table (last accessed February 12, 2018).

35. Statistics Sweden, http://www.statistikdatabasen.scb.se/pxweb/en/ssd/START__BE__BE0101__BE0101E/FodelselandArK/?rxid=7812b8b5-300e-4d9b-b731-2eceacc7fbb1 (last accessed February 12, 2018). Note: for a much more reader-friendly look at the statistics, go to the Wikipedia page "Immigration to Sweden" and scroll down to "Country of origin for persons born abroad." The information from the table there is taken from the above named website, but saves you a tremendous amount of calculation.

36. Census 2016, p.50 http://www.cso.ie/en/media/csoie/newsevents/documents/census2016summaryresultspart1/Census2016SummaryPart1.pdf (last accessed February 12, 2018).

37. Croatian Bureau of Statistics, "Population by Ethnicity, 1971-2011, Censuses," https://www.dzs.hr/Eng/censuses/census2011/results/htm/usp_03_EN.htm (last accessed February 12, 2018).

38. Statistics Estonia, "Quarterly Bulletin of *Statistics Estonia* 1/2017." P.53, file:///C:/Users/Owner/Downloads/Kvartalikiri_1_17%20 (1).pdf (last accessed February 12, 2018).

39. Julie Schindall, "Switzerland's non-EU Immigrants: Their Integration and Swiss Attitudes," Migration Policy Institute, https://www.migrationpolicy.org/article/switzerlands-non-eu-immigrants-their-integration-and-swiss-attitudes (last accessed February 13, 2018).

40. Federal Statistics Office, https://www.bfs.admin.ch/bfs/en/home/statistics/population/migration-integration/foreign.html (last accessed February 13, 2018).

41. Statista, "Number of foreigner in Austria after the ten most important nationalities on 1 January 2018," https://de.statista.com/statistik/daten/studie/293019/umfrage/auslaender-in-oesterreich-nach-staatsangehoerigkeit/ (last accessed February 13, 2018).

42. Statistics Luxembourg, http://www.statistiques.public.lu/fr/publications/series/livre-recensement-2011/structure-livre/index.html, Table 2.6 (last accessed February 13, 2018).

43. Wikipedia contributors, "Demographics of Liechtenstein," *Wikipedia, The Free Encyclopedia,* https://en.wikipedia.org/w/index.php?title=Demographics_of_Liechtenstein&oldid=799568969 (last accessed February 14, 2018).

44. General population Census 2008," https://web.archive.org/web/20110516232944/http://www.gouv.mc/devwww/wwwnew.nsf/e89a6190e96cbd1fc1256f7f005dbe6e/64a1643c86f9f661c12575ae004cc473/$FILE/Recensement2008_Ch1.pdf (last accessed February 12, 2018).

45. Elma Global residence and citizenship by investment, "Immigration to Andorra for High Net Worth Individuals," https://www.second-citizenship.org/publications-on-immigration-and-dual-citizenship/immigration-to-andorra-for-high-net-worth-individuals/ (last accessed February 12, 2018).

46. Global Slavery Index, https://www.globalslaveryindex.org/findings/ (last accessed February 14, 2018).

47. Annie Kelly, "European governments oblivious to forced labor conditions, says report," *The Guardian*, June 5, 2013, https://www.theguardian.com/global-development/2013/jun/05/european-governments-oblivious-forced-labour-conditions (last accessed February 15, 2018).

48. Aamna, Mohdin, "The most refugee-friendly country in Europe is growing weary," *Quartz Media*, September 7, 2016, https://qz.com/774427/the-most-refugee-friendly-country-in-europe-is-growing-weary/ (last accessed February 16, 2018).

49. World Happiness Report 2018, https://s3.amazonaws.com/happiness-report/2018/WHR_web.pdf (last accessed June 15, 2018).

50. United Nations Development Programme, "Human Development Index and its components," http://hdr.undp.org/en/composite/HDI (last accessed February 16, 2018).

51. OECD Better Life Index, http://www.oecdbetterlifeindex.org/ (last accessed February 16, 2018).

52. CAF World Giving Index 2017, September 2017, p.11, https://www.cafonline.org/docs/default-source/about-us-publications/cafworldgivingindex2017_2167a_web_210917.pdf?sfvrsn=ed1dac40_10 (last accessed February 16, 2018).

53. The Philanthropy Roundtable, http://www.philanthropyroundtable.org/almanac/statistics/ (last accessed February 18, 2018).

54. OECD, "Development Aid in 2015 continues to grow despite costs for in-donor refugees," April 13, 2016, http://www.oecd.org/dac/stats/ODA-2015-detailed-summary.pdf (last accessed February 18, 2018).

55. Simon Tomlinson, "Revealed: How immigrants in America are sending $120 BILLION to their struggling families back home," Daily Mail.com, January 31, 2013, http://www.dailymail

.co.uk/news/article-2271455/Revealed-How-immigrants-America-sending-120-BILLION-struggling-families-home.html (last accessed February 18, 2018).

56. Stephen J. Rose, "The Growing Size and Income of the Upper Middle Class," *Urban Institute*, June, 2016, https://www.urban.org/sites/default/files/publication/81581/2000819-The-Growing-Size-and-Incomes-of-the-Upper-Middle-Class.pdf (last accessed February 19, 2018).

57. Arthur Herman, *How the Scots Invented the Modern World* (New York: Three Rivers Press, 2001), pp.76-77.

58. Ibid, p.81.

59. Ibid, pp.82-83.

60. Walter Williams, *American Contempt for Liberty* (Stanford, CA: Hoover Institution Press, 2015), p.370.

61. Thomas Sowell, *Economic Facts and Fallacies* (New York: Basic Books, 2008), p.162.

62. Deirdre N. McCloskey, "The Formula for a Richer World? Equality, Liberty, Justice," *The New York Times*, September 2, 2016, https://www.nytimes.com/2016/09/04/upshot/the-formula-for-a-richer-world-equality-liberty-justice.html (last accessed February 21, 2018).

63. Matt Ridley, *The Rational Optimist* (New York: HarperCollins, 2010), pp. 320-321.

64. "Better and Better," *The Economist*, September 3, 2016, p.70.

65. Robert Sapolsky, *Behave: The Biology of Humans at Our Best and Worst* (New York: Penguin Press, 2017), p.617.

66. Drew Desilver, "U.S. students' academic achievement still lags that of their peers in many other countries," Pew Research Center, February 15, 2017, http://www.pewresearch.org/fact-tank/2017/02/15/u-s-students-internationally-math-science/ (last accessed June 16, 2018).

67. Jonathan Rabinovits, "Poor ranking on international tests misleading about U.S. performance, new report finds," Stanford Graduate School of Education, January 15, 2013, https://ed.stanford.edu/news/poor-ranking-international-tests-misleading-about-us-performance-new-report-finds (last accessed June 16, 2018).

68. Ibid. (last accessed June 16, 2018).

69. Ibid. (last accessed June 16, 2018).

70. Canadian Union of Public Employees, "Spotlight: Census shows racial pay gaps persist," December 12, 2017, https://cupe.ca/spotlight-census-shows-racial-pay-gaps-persist (last accessed June 16, 2018).

71. Omar Khan, "The racial wealth gap: not just an American problem," Reuters.com, April 8, 2011, http://blogs.reuters.com/great-debate-uk/2011/04/08/the-racial-wealth-gap-not-just-an-american-problem/ (last accessed June 16, 2018).

72. Rabinovits (last accessed June 16, 2018).

73. World Economic Forum, "6 charts on education around the world," September 25, 2017, https://www.weforum.org/agenda/2017/09/countries-with-best-education-systems/ (last accessed February 22, 2018).

74. Richard Sander and Stuart Taylor, Jr., *Mismatch* (New York: Basic Books, 2012), location 4639 of 7117, Kindle.

75. CWUR – World University Rankings, http://cwur.org/2017.php (last accessed February 22, 2018).

76. Times Higher Education, "World University Rankings 2018," https://www.timeshighereducation.com/world-university-rankings/2018/world-ranking#!/page/0/length/25/sort_by/rank/sort_order/asc/cols/stats (last accessed February 22, 2018).

77. The World Food Prize, https://www.worldfoodprize.org/en/dr_norman_e_borlaug/extended_biography/ (last accessed February 22, 2018).

78. "The Probability of Collisions with Earth," Jet Propulsion Laboratories, https://www2.jpl.nasa.gov/sl9/back2.html (last accessed March 19, 2018).

79. Phil Plait, When Will the Earth Get Hit by Another Asteroid?" *SLATE*, February 13, 2014, http://www.slate.com/articles/health_and_science/mysteries_of_the_universe/2014/02/anniversary_of_chelyabinsk_asteroid_impact_we_need_to_test_a_deflector_mission.html (last accessed March 19, 2018).

80. Ibid. (last accessed March 19, 2018).

81. Charles Q. Choi, "How Weather Satellites Changed the World," SPACE.com, April 13, 2010, https://www.space.com/8186-weather-satellites-changed-world.html (last accessed March 19, 2018).

82. Mary Beth Griggs, "NOAA's satellites are on the chopping block. Here's why we need them," *Popular Science*, March 6, 2017, https://www.popsci.com/what-do-noaa-satellites-do?dom=rss-default&src=syn (last accessed March 19, 2018).

83. Jeremy Hsu, "The U.S. Is About to Get Much Better Weather Satellites," *Scientific American*, October 1, 2016, https://www.scientificamerican.com/article/the-u-s-is-about-to-get-much-better-weather-satellites/ (last accessed March 19, 2018).

84. Christopher Jencks, "The War on Poverty: Was It Lost?" *The New York Review of Books*, April 2, 2015, http://www.nybooks.com/articles/2015/04/02/war-poverty-was-it-lost/ (last accessed February 22, 2018).

85. Tim Worstall, "The True US Poverty Rate Is 4.5%, Not 14.5%," *Forbes*, March 15, 2015, https://www.forbes.com/sites/timworstall/2015/03/15/the-true-us-poverty-rate-is-4-5-not-14-5/#6d9f46f5571f (last accessed February 22, 2018).

86. Jencks, "The War on Poverty."

87. Gallup, "U.S. Satisfaction Higher Among Blacks, Hispanics Than Whites," July 15, 2016, http://news.gallup.com/poll/193721/satisfaction-higher-among-blacks-hispanics-whites.aspx (last accessed February 24, 2018).

88. Jeff Jacoby, "When America's melting pot works," *Boston Globe*, September 1, 2017, https://www.bostonglobe.com/opinion/2017/09/01/when-america-melting-pot-works/xGCMb2tmSgbPYpee-aqUN4H/story.html (last accessed February 25, 2018).

89. U.S. Department of Justice Federal Bureau of Investigation, "2016 Hate Crime Statistics," https://ucr.fbi.gov/hate-crime/2016/tables/table-1 (last accessed February 25, 2018).

90. FBI, "What We Investigate," https://www.fbi.gov/investigate/civil-rights/hate-crimes (last accessed February 25, 2018).

91. Statistics Canada, "Police-reported hate crime, 2016," https://www.statcan.gc.ca/daily-quotidien/171128/dq171128d-eng.htm (last accessed February 25, 2018).

92. Josh Dehaas, "What counts as a 'hate crime' in Canada?" CTV News, March 1, 2017, https://www.ctvnews.ca/canada/what-counts-as-a-hate-crime-in-canada-1.3307395 (last accessed February 25, 2018).

93. May Bullman, "Antisemitic hate crimes hit record high as violent assaults increase by more than a third in a year," *Independent*, February 1, 2018, http://www.independent.co.uk/news/uk/crime/antisemitic-hate-crimes-record-high-violent-assaults-community-security-trust-cst-a8187941.html (last accessed February 25, 2018).

94. Noam Schimmel, "French Response to Anti-Jewish Racism, Bigotry and Discrimination: The 'loneliness' of French Jews," Humanity in Action, https://www.humanityinaction.org/knowledgebase/688-french-responses-to-anti-jewish-racism-bigotry-and-discrimination-the-loneliness-of-french-jews (last accessed February 28, 2018).

95. The figures for the number of violent attacks against Jews comes from Johannes Due Enstad, "Antisemitic Violence in Europe, 2005-2015," https://www.hlsenteret.no/publikasjoner/digitale-hef ter/antisemittisk-vold-i-europa_engelsk_endelig-versjon.pdf (last accessed February 28, 2018). The figures for the number of Jews in each country comes from the Institute for Jewish Policy Research, http://www.jpr.org.uk/map (last accessed February 28, 2018). From those figures I calculated the number of attacks per 100,000.

96. Ibid (last accessed February 28, 2018).

97. Bruce Bawer, *While Europe Slept: How Radical Islam Is Destroying the West From Within* (New York: Broadway Books, 2006), pp. 6-7.

98. Ibid, pp. 11-13.

99. Ibid, pp. 45-46.

100. Ibid, pp. 55-56, 70.

101. John Stossell, *No, They Can't* (New York: Threshold Editions, 2012), p. 113.

102. Brian Crowley, "The Top Ten Things People Believe About Canadian Health Care, But Shouldn't," The Heritage Foundation, November 10, 2004, https://www.heritage.org/health-care-reform /report/the-top-ten-things-people-believe-about-canadian-health-care-shouldnt (last accessed June 19, 2018).

103. Scott W. Atlas, *In Excellent Health: Setting the Record Straight on America's Health Care* (Stanford, CA: Hoover Institution Press, 2011), p. 82.

104. Bruce Bawer, email message to author, February 8, 2018.

105. Central Intelligence Agency The World Factbook, https:// www.cia.gov/library/publications/the-world-factbook/rankorder/ 2102rank.html Note: one must take out "The European Union" when counting "countries,"(last accessed February 28, 2018).

106. Central Intelligence Agency The World Factbook, https:// www.cia.gov/library/publications/the-world-factbook/rankorder/ 2091rank.html Note: one must take out "The European Union" when counting "countries," (last accessed February 28, 2018).

107. OECD, "Obesity Update 2017," https://www.oecd.org/els/ health-systems/Obesity-Update-2017.pdf (last accessed February 28, 2018).

108. Atlas, *In Excellent Health*, pp. 111-112.

109. Ibid, pp. 113-114, 116.

110. Ibid, pp. 121-122.

111. Ibid, pp. 129, 132-133.

112. Ibid, p. 164.

113. Ibid, p. 223.

114. Ibid, pp. 223-224, 226.

115. Stossel, *No, they Can't*, p. 116.

116. Atlas, *In Excellent Health*, p. 209.

117. Tara Haelle, "U.S. infant mortality rate worse than other countries," CBS News, September 24, 2014, https://www.cbsnews. com/news/u-s-infant-mortality-rate-worse-than-other-countries/ (last accessed March 1, 2018).

118. Scott W. Atlas, "Infant Mortality: A Deceptive Statistic," *National Review*, September 14, 2011, https://www.nationalreview.com/2011/09/infant-mortality-deceptive-statistic-scott-w-atlas/ (last accessed March 1, 2018).

119. Haidt, *The Righteous Mind*, pp. 354-356.

120. Marty Nemko, "Men, Power, Money, and Sex: An interview with men's advocate, Warren Farrell," *Psychology Today*, July 17, 2014, https://www.psychologytoday.com/blog/how-do-life/201407/men-power-money-and-sex (last accessed June 20, 2018).

121. American Foundation for Suicide Prevention, "Suicide Statistics," https://afsp.org/about-suicide/suicide-statistics/ (last accessed March 8, 2018).
122. Marty Nemko, "Should We Pay More Attention to Men's Health?" http://www.martynemko.com/articles/should-we-pay-more-attention-mens-health_id1231 (last accessed March 1, 2018).
123. Bureau of Labor Statistics, "National Census of Fatal Occupational Injuries in 2016," December 19, 2017, https://www.bls.gov/news.release/pdf/cfoi.pdf (last accessed March 1, 2018).
124. Lily Rothman, "Exclusive New 'Happiness Index' Number Reveals How Americans Feel Right Now," *TIME*, July 1, 2016, http://time.com/4389726/harris-poll-happiness-index-2016/ (last accessed March 1, 2018).
125. Brett Arends, "The idea of the 'gender pay gap' is mostly bogus," MarketWatch, April 14, 2016, https://www.marketwatch.com/story/the-idea-of-the-gender-pay-gap-is-mostly-bogus-2016-04-14 (last accessed March 1, 2018).
126. Sowell, *Economic Facts and Fallacies*, pp. 65-68, 70, 85.
127. Diana Furchgott-Roth, "Are Women Paid Less than Men?" Manhattan Institute Issues 2016, p.3, https://www.manhattan-institute.org/sites/default/files/IB-DFR-0416.pdf (last accessed March 1, 2018).
128. Diana Furchgott-Roth, "The gender wage gap is a myth," MarketWatch, July 26, 2012, https://www.marketwatch.com/story/the-gender-wage-gap-is-a-myth-2012-07-26 (last accessed March 1, 2018).
129. Marina N. Bolotnikova, "Reassessing the Gender Wage Gap," *Harvard Magazine*, May-June, 2016, https://harvardmagazine.com/2016/05/reassessing-the-gender-wage-gap (last accessed March 1, 2018).
130. Sowell, *Economic Facts and Fallacies*, p. 78.

131. Natalia A. Kolesnikova and Yang Liu, "Gender Wage Gap May Be Much Smaller Than Most Think," Federal Reserve Bank of St. Louis, October 2011, https://www.stlouisfed.org/publications/regional-economist/october-2011/gender-wage-gap-may-be-much-smaller-than-most-think (last accessed March 1, 2018).
132. Christina Hoff Summers, *The War Against Boys* (New York: Simon and Schuster, 2013), p. 26.
133. Bert H. Hoff, J.D., "CDC Study: More Men than Women Victims of Partner Abuse," http://www.saveservices.org/2012/02/cdc-study-more-men-than-women-victims-of-partner-abuse/ Note: SAVE is an acronym for Stop Abusive and Violent Environments (last accessed March 1, 2018).
134. Denis Canpbell, "More than 40% of domestic violence victims are male, report reveals," *Guardian*, September 4, 2010, https://www.theguardian.com/society/2010/sep/05/men-victims-domestic-violence (last accessed March 2, 2018).
135. Conor Friedersdorf, "The Understudied Female Sexual Predator," *The Atlantic*, November 28, 2016, https://www.theatlantic.com/science/archive/2016/11/the-understudied-female-sexual-predator/503492/ (last accessed March 2, 2018).
136. Ibid (last accessed March 2, 2018).
137. Ibid (last accessed March 2, 2018).
138. Statista, "Number of bachelor's degrees earned in the United States from 1949/50 to 2026/27 by gender (in 1,000), https://www.statista.com/statistics/185157/number-of-bachelor-degrees-by-gender-since-1950/ (last accessed March 2, 2018).
139. Dr. Michael W. Kirst, "Women Earn More Degrees Than Men; Gap Keeps Increasing," Stanford/The College Puzzle, May 28, 2013, https://collegepuzzle.stanford.edu/women-earn-more-degrees-than-men-gap-keeps-increasing/ (last accessed March 2, 2018).

140. Sonja Starr, "Estimating Gender Disparities in Federal Criminal Cases," University of Michigan Law School, August 1, 2012, https://repository.law.umich.edu/cgi/viewcontent.cgi?referer =https://www.google.com/&httpsredir=1&article=1164&context =law_econ_current (last accessed March 2, 2018).
141. Marty Nemko, "The Problem With Boys: An ignored crisis," *Psychology Today*, September 22, 2014, https://www. psychologytoday.com/blog/how-do-life/201409/the-problem-boys (last accessed March 2, 2018).
142. Rob Whitley, "Is There Really a Boy Crisis?" *Psychology Today*, June 22, 2017, https://www.psychologytoday.com/blog/talking-about-men/201706/is-there-really-boy-crisis (last accessed March 2, 2018).
143. Summers, *The War Against Boys*, pp. 156-157.
144. Ibid, pp. 35-38.
145. Ibid, p. 43.
146. Ibid, pp. 40-41.
147. Ibid, p. 74.
148. Freedom House, "About Freedom in the World: An annual study of political rights and civil liberties," https://freedomhouse. org/report-types/freedom-world (last accessed March 2, 2018).
149. Robert Kagan, "The Allure of Normalcy," *The New Republic*, June 9, 2014, p. 22.
150. Ibid, p. 25.
151. Robert Kagan, *The World America Made* (New York: Vintage Books, 2012), p. 55.
152. Samuel P. Huntington, *The Third Wave: Democratization in the Late Twentieth Century* (Norman, Oklahoma: University of Oklahoma Press, 1993), location 1557 of 6895, Kindle.

Acknowledgments

While not pretending that they would agree with everything I have written (a year from today *I* might not agree with everything I have written, because of exposure to evidence of which I'm not aware – or to new evidence), I would like to thank Bruce Bawer and Jon VanZile for their encouragement in writing this book. I would also like to recommend Editing for Authors (www.editing-forauthors.com) to anyone interested in help with self-publishing. The author can be reached at phkershner@yahoo.com

As an independent author, word-of-mouth is my best advertising. If you have found this book to be helpful, I would appreciate it if you would let others know. Finally, if you're so inclined, a brief review on Amazon would be a huge help.

Many thanks,
Phil